# The China Economic Experiment: A Success Story of Capitalism in a Communist Regime

Copyright Page

TITLE: The China Economic Experiment: A Success Story of Capitalism in a Communist Regime

1<sup>ST</sup> Edition



ISBN: 9798223414711

# Table of Contents

The China Economic Experiment: A Success Story of Capitalism in a Communist Regime

By Roberto Miguel Rodriguez

# Chapter 1: The Successes of the China Economic Experiment: Using a Capitalist Economic System in a Communist Dictatorship

The Evolution of China's Economic Model

China's economic model has undergone a remarkable transformation over the past few decades. From a planned economy under the rule of a communist regime, China has successfully implemented market-oriented reforms that have propelled its economic growth and positioned it as a major player in the global economy. This subchapter explores the key aspects of this evolution and its implications for the future development of China.

One of the main successes of the China economic experiment has been the effective utilization of a capitalist economic system within a communist dictatorship. This unique combination has allowed China to harness the benefits of market-oriented reforms while maintaining political stability and control. The success of this model has attracted the attention of economists, politicians, diplomats, and scholars worldwide, who are eager to understand the factors behind China's economic achievements.

Market-oriented reforms have played a crucial role in China's economic growth. By liberalizing trade and investment policies, China has been able to attract foreign investments, which have served as catalysts for its economic transformation. The inflow of foreign capital, technology, and expertise has not only boosted China's productivity and industrial capabilities but also facilitated its integration into the global economy.

Special Economic Zones (SEZs) have been instrumental in China's economic success. These designated areas, characterized by preferential policies and incentives, have acted as testing grounds for market-oriented reforms. SEZs have attracted foreign investments, promoted export-oriented industries, and served as models for economic reforms in other parts of the country.

The integration of state-owned enterprises (SOEs) into a capitalist economic system has been a significant milestone in China's economic development. The restructuring and corporatization of SOEs have increased their efficiency and competitiveness, while also opening up opportunities for private sector participation and entrepreneurship.

China's economic model has witnessed the rapid development of entrepreneurship and the private sector. The government's support for small and medium-sized enterprises (SMEs) has fostered innovation, job creation, and technological advancements. The rise of a vibrant private sector has contributed to China's economic dynamism and resilience.

The transition from a planned to a market economy has brought about both challenges and opportunities for China. While the opening up of markets and the embrace of market forces have unleashed the country's economic potential, they have also led to income inequality and social disparities. Addressing these issues remains a priority for China's policymakers.

Innovation and technological advancements have been key drivers of China's economic achievements. The country's focus on research and development, coupled with its emphasis on education and human capital development, has enabled China to become a global leader in areas such as artificial intelligence, renewable energy, and e-commerce.

Globalization has played a pivotal role in China's economic experiment. By embracing international trade and investment, China has been able to leverage its competitive advantage in manufacturing and become the world's largest exporter. At the same time, China's integration into the global economy has exposed it to external risks and challenges, requiring careful management and adaptation.

The sustainability of China's economic model and its implications for future development are subjects of intense debate. While China has achieved remarkable economic growth, questions remain about the long-term viability of its model, including issues related to environmental sustainability, debt levels, and social stability. Addressing these challenges will be critical for China's continued success.

In conclusion, the evolution of China's economic model from a planned to a market economy has been a remarkable success story. The use of a capitalist economic system within a communist regime, market-oriented reforms, foreign investments, SEZs, the integration of SOEs, the development of entrepreneurship and the private sector, and the role of innovation and globalization have all played crucial roles in China's economic transformation. However, challenges such as income inequality, sustainability, and social disparities must be addressed for China to sustain its economic achievements and ensure future development.

The Role of State Planning in China's Economic Success

In the realm of economic development, China's success story stands out as a remarkable example of how a communist regime can effectively utilize a capitalist economic system to achieve unprecedented growth. This subchapter will delve into the crucial role played by state planning in China's economic success, examining how it has shaped and guided the country's transformation.

China's economic experiment began with market-oriented reforms, initiated by Deng Xiaoping in the late 1970s. These reforms aimed to introduce elements of capitalism into the centrally planned economy, and one of the key tools used to achieve this was state planning. The Chinese government, through its centralized planning mechanisms, played a pivotal role in guiding and directing the country's economic development.

Foreign investments have played a critical role in China's economic transformation, and state planning has been instrumental in attracting and channeling these investments effectively. The government has strategically utilized Special Economic Zones (SEZs) to attract foreign capital, technology, and expertise, creating a conducive environment for economic growth and development.

State-owned enterprises (SOEs) have also been integrated into China's capitalist economic system through state planning. The government has restructured and modernized these enterprises, allowing them to operate more efficiently and compete in the global market. State planning has facilitated the transformation of SOEs into competitive entities, contributing significantly to China's economic success.

Furthermore, China's economic development has been fueled by the growth of entrepreneurship and the private sector, which state planning has actively supported. The government has implemented policies that encourage the development of small and medium-sized enterprises, fostering innovation and creating new opportunities for economic growth.

The transition from a planned to a market economy has presented both challenges and opportunities for China. State planning has played a critical role in managing this transition, ensuring a smooth shift while addressing potential risks and uncertainties. The government has devised policies and implemented reforms to promote market competition, enhance regulatory frameworks, and establish a level playing field for businesses.

Innovation and technological advancements have been vital drivers of China's economic achievements, and state planning has actively supported these areas. The government has invested heavily in research and development, fostering a culture of innovation and providing incentives for technological advancements. This has propelled China to become a global leader in various industries, from telecommunications to renewable energy.

Globalization has had a profound impact on China's economic experiment, and state planning has been instrumental in navigating the challenges and opportunities it presents. The government has actively engaged in international trade and investment, promoting economic integration and forging strategic partnerships. State planning has helped China become an integral player in the global economy, contributing to its economic success.

However, China's capitalist-communist hybrid system has also led to income inequality and social disparities. State planning must address these issues to ensure a more equitable distribution of wealth and opportunities, fostering social cohesion and sustainable development.

The sustainability of China's economic model and its implications for future development are of paramount importance. State planning will continue to play a crucial role in guiding China's economic growth, ensuring sustainable development, and addressing environmental challenges. The government's commitment to long-term planning and strategic foresight will be vital in maintaining China's economic success while safeguarding its future.

In conclusion, state planning has been a cornerstone of China's economic success. It has guided and shaped the country's transformation, attracting foreign investments, integrating SOEs into a capitalist system, promoting entrepreneurship and innovation, managing the transition to a market economy, and seizing the opportunities of globalization. State planning will remain essential in addressing challenges, promoting sustainability, and securing China's future as a global economic powerhouse.

Market-oriented Reforms: A Catalyst for Growth

Market-oriented reforms have played a pivotal role in driving China's unprecedented economic growth and transforming it into a global economic powerhouse. This subchapter explores the various aspects of market-oriented reforms and their impact on China's economic success.

One of the key factors contributing to the success of the China economic experiment is the utilization of a capitalist economic system within a communist regime. This unique approach has allowed China to harness the benefits of market forces while maintaining political control. This subchapter delves into the successes of this experiment, highlighting how China's economic growth has outpaced that of many other countries.

Foreign investments have been instrumental in China's economic transformation. This subchapter examines the role of foreign investments in driving economic growth, attracting capital, technology, and expertise into the country. It also explores how China has leveraged these investments to its advantage and become a global manufacturing hub.

Special Economic Zones (SEZs) have been a crucial catalyst for China's economic success. This subchapter analyzes the influence of SEZs in promoting economic growth, attracting foreign investments, and fostering innovation. It also discusses how SEZs have served as testbeds for market-oriented reforms and played a vital role in China's economic transformation.

Integrating state-owned enterprises (SOEs) into a capitalist economic system has been a challenging but essential aspect of China's economic experiment. This subchapter explores the development of SOEs and the efforts made to introduce market-oriented reforms in these state-owned entities.

The emergence of entrepreneurship and the growth of the private sector have been significant drivers of China's economic success. This subchapter delves into the development of entrepreneurship and the private sector in China's economy, highlighting the opportunities and challenges faced by entrepreneurs in a rapidly changing business environment.

China's transition from a planned to a market economy has presented both challenges and opportunities. This subchapter discusses the various obstacles encountered during this transition and explores the potential benefits that a market-oriented economy can bring.

Innovation and technological advancements have played a pivotal role in China's economic achievements. This subchapter examines the role of innovation in driving economic growth and discusses the policies and initiatives implemented by the Chinese government to foster innovation and technological advancements.

Globalization has had a profound impact on China's economic experiment. This subchapter analyzes the influence of globalization on China's economic growth, trade patterns, and integration into the global economy.

Income inequality and social disparities have emerged as significant challenges in China's capitalist-communist hybrid system. This subchapter delves into the implications of income inequality, analyzes the efforts made by the Chinese government to address this issue, and explores potential solutions.

Finally, this subchapter reflects on the sustainability of China's economic model and its implications for future development. It explores the challenges and opportunities that lie ahead and discusses the potential paths China may take to ensure continued economic growth and stability.

The Impact of Economic Liberalization on Poverty Alleviation

In the subchapter titled "The Impact of Economic Liberalization on Poverty Alleviation" from the book "The China Economic Experiment: A Success Story of Capitalism in a Communist Regime," we explore the profound implications of market-oriented reforms on poverty reduction in China. This chapter delves into the various elements of China's economic liberalization and highlights the role they played in lifting millions out of poverty.

China's transition from a planned to a market economy has been instrumental in driving its impressive economic growth and poverty reduction. The introduction of market-oriented reforms unleashed the potential of entrepreneurship and the private sector, creating new opportunities for economic advancement. The development of a vibrant private sector has played a crucial role in job creation, increasing incomes, and reducing poverty levels across the country.

Foreign investments have also played a significant role in China's economic transformation. By attracting foreign capital and expertise, China was able to accelerate its industrialization and modernization processes. This influx of foreign investments has not only stimulated economic growth but has also contributed to poverty alleviation through the creation of new jobs and the transfer of knowledge and technology.

Special Economic Zones (SEZs) have emerged as crucial catalysts for China's economic success. These designated areas, characterized by preferential policies and incentives, have attracted both domestic and foreign investments, fostering economic growth and poverty reduction. SEZs have acted as laboratories for experimentation, promoting innovation, and driving economic reforms that have had a positive impact on poverty alleviation.

The integration of state-owned enterprises (SOEs) into a capitalist economic system has also played a significant role in poverty reduction. By subjecting these enterprises to market forces and competition, China was able to increase efficiency, productivity, and profitability. The transformation of SOEs not only helped boost economic growth but also generated resources that could be used for poverty alleviation programs and social welfare initiatives.

Technological advancements and innovation have been key drivers of China's economic achievements. The country's focus on research and development, coupled with its commitment to technological advancements, has allowed China to become a global leader in various sectors. Technological progress has not only fueled economic growth but has also created new opportunities for poverty reduction by enabling the development of high-value industries and the creation of skilled jobs.

However, China's economic experiment has not been without challenges. Income inequality and social disparities have emerged as pressing issues in China's capitalist-communist hybrid system. While poverty levels have significantly decreased, the gap between the rich and the poor has widened, posing challenges to social cohesion and stability.

The sustainability of China's economic model and its implications for future development also warrant careful consideration. As China strives to maintain its economic growth and continue poverty alleviation efforts, it must address environmental concerns, promote inclusive growth, and ensure equitable distribution of resources.

In conclusion, the impact of economic liberalization on poverty alleviation in China has been substantial. Market-oriented reforms, foreign investments, Special Economic Zones, the integration of state-owned enterprises, and technological advancements have all played vital roles in lifting millions out of poverty. However, challenges such as income inequality and sustainability remain, necessitating further reforms and policy adjustments to ensure continued progress in the quest for poverty eradication.

# Chapter 2: The Impact of Market-oriented Reforms on China's Economic Growth

Opening up to Foreign Trade and Investment

In the ever-evolving landscape of globalization, China's decision to open up its economy to foreign trade and investment has played a pivotal role in its remarkable economic transformation. This subchapter delves into the various aspects of this momentous shift, exploring its impact on China's economic growth, the role of foreign investments, the influence of Special Economic Zones (SEZs), the integration of state-owned enterprises (SOEs), the development of entrepreneurship and the private sector, and the challenges and opportunities of transitioning from a planned to a market economy.

The success story of the China economic experiment lies in its adept utilization of a capitalist economic system within a communist regime. This unique model has defied conventional wisdom and surpassed expectations, drawing the attention of economists, politicians, diplomats, and scholars alike. By embracing market-oriented reforms, China has managed to achieve unprecedented levels of economic growth. The subchapter analyzes the factors that have contributed to this growth, such as the liberalization of trade and investment policies, the ease of doing business, and the emphasis on innovation and technological advancements.

Foreign investments have played a crucial role in China's economic transformation. The subchapter explores the impact of these investments on various sectors, including manufacturing, infrastructure, and services. It also highlights the significance of Special Economic Zones, which have acted as engines of growth by attracting foreign investments, promoting exports, and facilitating technology transfers. These zones have been instrumental in the success of China's economic experiment, serving as testing grounds for market-oriented reforms and fostering entrepreneurial spirit.

The integration of state-owned enterprises into a capitalist economic system has been a key aspect of China's economic transition. This subchapter examines the challenges and opportunities associated with this process, including restructuring, privatization, and the need for improved corporate governance. It also explores the development of entrepreneurship and the private sector, highlighting their vital role in driving innovation, job creation, and economic diversification.

The subchapter also addresses the challenges and opportunities that arise from China's transition from a planned to a market economy. It explores the implications of income inequality and social disparities within China's hybrid system and discusses strategies to mitigate these issues. Additionally, it examines the sustainability of China's economic model and its implications for future development, particularly in the face of global economic uncertainties.

In conclusion, the opening up of China's economy to foreign trade and investment has been a pivotal factor in its economic success story. By leveraging market-oriented reforms, attracting foreign investments, nurturing entrepreneurship, and integrating state-owned enterprises into a capitalist system, China has achieved unprecedented levels of growth and development. However, challenges remain, such as income inequality and the need for sustainable development. Understanding the dynamics of China's economic experiment is essential for economists, politicians, diplomats, scholars, and anyone interested in the complexities of a capitalist economic system within a communist regime.

Privatization and Deregulation: Unleashing Entrepreneurial Spirit

In the book "The China Economic Experiment: A Success Story of Capitalism in a Communist Regime," one of the key subchapters addresses the topic of "Privatization and Deregulation: Unleashing Entrepreneurial Spirit." This subchapter explores the pivotal role played by market-oriented reforms, foreign investments, and the integration of state-owned enterprises (SOEs) into a capitalist economic system in China's remarkable economic transformation.

China's economic experiment has been characterized by the use of a capitalist economic system within the framework of a communist dictatorship. The successes of this experiment can be attributed to the implementation of market-oriented reforms, which have gradually dismantled the centralized planning system and introduced elements of competition and entrepreneurship. Through privatization and deregulation, China has created an environment that fosters innovation, investment, and economic growth.

Foreign investments have played a significant role in China's economic transformation. The country has actively sought foreign capital and technology, creating partnerships and encouraging multinational corporations to establish a presence in the country. This has not only boosted economic growth but also facilitated the transfer of knowledge and technology, contributing to China's rapid industrialization and modernization.

Special Economic Zones (SEZs) have been instrumental in China's economic success. These designated areas, characterized by reduced regulations and preferential policies, have attracted both domestic and foreign investors. SEZs have served as incubators for entrepreneurship and innovation, allowing businesses to thrive and drive economic growth.

The integration of state-owned enterprises into a capitalist economic system has also been crucial. China has implemented reforms to make

SOEs more efficient and competitive, allowing them to operate in a market-oriented manner. This integration has not only improved the performance of these enterprises but has also created new opportunities for private businesses and entrepreneurs.

Furthermore, the development of entrepreneurship and the private sector have been key drivers of China's economic growth. As the economy opened up, individuals and businesses were given greater freedom to pursue their entrepreneurial ambitions. This has resulted in the emergence of a vibrant private sector, contributing to job creation, innovation, and economic diversification.

While China's transition from a planned to a market economy has presented challenges, it has also opened up opportunities for growth and development. The country has had to navigate issues such as income inequality and social disparities, but efforts have been made to address these through inclusive policies and social welfare programs.

China's economic achievements have also been fueled by a focus on innovation and technological advancements. The country has invested heavily in research and development, resulting in significant breakthroughs in areas such as artificial intelligence, renewable energy, and telecommunications. These advancements have not only bolstered economic growth but have also positioned China as a global leader in technological innovation.

Globalization has played a significant role in China's economic experiment. The country has embraced global trade and actively sought to integrate into the global economy. This has allowed China to tap into international markets, attract foreign investment, and expand its export capabilities.

However, China's capitalist-communist hybrid system has also led to income inequality and social disparities. As the private sector has thrived, some segments of society have benefited more than others. Efforts are being made to address these issues through targeted policies aimed at reducing poverty and promoting inclusive growth.

The sustainability of China's economic model and its implications for future development remain a topic of debate. As the country continues to navigate its economic transition, it will need to address challenges such as environmental sustainability, financial stability, and geopolitical tensions. Nonetheless, China's economic experiment has demonstrated the potential for a capitalist economic system to coexist with a communist regime, paving the way for future discussions and experiments in other parts of the world.

In conclusion, the subchapter "Privatization and Deregulation: Unleashing Entrepreneurial Spirit" delves into the key factors that have contributed to China's economic success. Market-oriented reforms, foreign investments, special economic zones, the integration of state-owned enterprises, the development of entrepreneurship and the private sector, and the role of innovation and globalization have all played a pivotal role in China's transformation from a planned to a market economy. However, challenges such as income inequality and sustainability must be addressed to ensure the continued success and future development of China's economic model.

The Transformation of Agriculture: From Communes to Household Responsibility System

Introduction:

The transformation of agriculture from communes to the household responsibility system was a pivotal moment in China's economic experiment. This subchapter explores the profound impact of this reform on China's agricultural sector and its broader implications for the country's economic development. Addressing economists, politicians, diplomats, and scholars, this chapter delves into the successes, challenges, and opportunities that arose from this transformation.

Historical Context:

Under Mao Zedong's leadership, China had implemented a collective farming system known as communes. While this system initially aimed to increase agricultural productivity, it soon became apparent that it stifled individual incentives and hindered economic growth. As China sought to modernize its economy, Deng Xiaoping introduced market-oriented reforms, including the household responsibility system, in the late 1970s.

The Household Responsibility System:

The household responsibility system marked a significant departure from the collective farming model. It granted individual households the right to cultivate and sell their own agricultural products, thereby providing farmers with greater autonomy and incentives to increase productivity. This decentralized approach revolutionized China's agricultural sector, leading to a surge in output and improved living standards for rural communities.

Implications for Economic Growth:

The market-oriented reforms in agriculture had far-reaching effects on China's overall economic growth. The increased productivity and surplus generated by the agricultural sector fueled industrialization and urbanization. As surplus labor migrated from rural areas to cities, it provided a workforce for China's burgeoning manufacturing sector, contributing to the country's rapid economic expansion.

Foreign Investments and Special Economic Zones (SEZs):

Foreign investments played a crucial role in China's economic transformation, particularly in the agricultural sector. The government encouraged foreign companies to invest in agriculture, leveraging their expertise and technology to modernize farming practices. Additionally, the establishment of Special Economic Zones (SEZs) allowed for experimentation with market-oriented policies, attracting foreign investors and stimulating agricultural development.

Integration of State-Owned Enterprises (SOEs):

The transformation of agriculture also necessitated the integration of state-owned enterprises (SOEs) into a capitalist economic system. SOEs in the agricultural sector underwent restructuring, adopting market-oriented practices to increase efficiency and competitiveness. This integration facilitated the flow of resources between the agricultural and industrial sectors, contributing to overall economic growth.

Challenges and Opportunities:

China's transition from a planned to a market economy presented both challenges and opportunities. The shift in agricultural practices required significant adjustments, such as land redistribution and education and training programs for farmers. However, this transition also created new opportunities for entrepreneurship and the development of a thriving private sector, which further propelled economic growth.

Conclusion:

The transformation of agriculture from communes to the household responsibility system revolutionized China's economic landscape. This reform unlocked the agricultural sector's potential, fueling industrialization, urbanization, and overall economic growth. The integration of foreign investments, SEZs, and state-owned enterprises played instrumental roles in this transformation. Despite challenges, China's transition to a market economy has created a sustainable economic model with implications for future development. As the country continues to innovate and embrace technological advancements, it remains a unique case study for economists, politicians, diplomats, and scholars interested in the successes and challenges of combining capitalism and communism.

Industrialization and Urbanization: Engines of Economic Expansion

As we delve into the remarkable success story of the China Economic Experiment, it becomes evident that industrialization and urbanization have played pivotal roles in driving the country's economic expansion. This subchapter aims to shed light on the various aspects of this transformation, discussing the impact of market-oriented reforms, foreign investments, Special Economic Zones (SEZs), state-owned enterprises (SOEs), entrepreneurship, private sector development, innovation, technological advancements, globalization, income inequality, social disparities, and the sustainability of China's economic model.

China's economic growth can be largely attributed to the market-oriented reforms initiated in the late 1970s. These reforms marked a significant departure from the centrally planned economic system, embracing elements of a capitalist economy within a communist regime. By allowing market forces to operate and encouraging private enterprise, China unleashed the entrepreneurial spirit of its citizens, leading to a surge in economic activity and unprecedented growth rates.

Foreign investments have also played a crucial role in China's economic transformation. The country's open-door policy and attractive investment incentives have attracted multinational corporations seeking to tap into the vast Chinese market. These investments have not only provided capital and technology but also facilitated the transfer of managerial skills and best practices, fueling China's industrialization and urbanization.

The establishment of Special Economic Zones (SEZs) in the 1980s further accelerated China's economic success. These designated areas offered preferential tax incentives, relaxed regulations, and easier access to foreign capital, attracting both domestic and foreign investments. The SEZs served as experimental grounds, showcasing the benefits of market-oriented reforms and providing a springboard for the broader economic transformation.

The integration of state-owned enterprises (SOEs) into a capitalist economic system has been a significant challenge for China. While some SOEs have successfully transformed into competitive entities, others have struggled to adapt to market forces. The government's ongoing efforts to reform and restructure these enterprises have been critical in improving efficiency and promoting healthy competition.

China's economic model has also witnessed a remarkable growth in entrepreneurship and the private sector. The rise of small and medium-sized enterprises (SMEs) has contributed significantly to job creation, innovation, and economic diversification. The government's support for entrepreneurship and the removal of regulatory barriers have fostered a vibrant ecosystem for startups and private businesses.

Innovation and technological advancements have been key drivers of China's economic achievements. The country has made substantial investments in research and development, resulting in breakthroughs in various sectors such as telecommunications, renewable energy, artificial intelligence, and e-commerce. China's ability to adapt and leverage technology has significantly enhanced its competitiveness in the global marketplace.

Globalization has played a dual role in China's economic experiment. On one hand, it has provided access to foreign markets, technology, and capital, enabling Chinese companies to expand their global footprint. On the other hand, it has exposed China to increased competition and challenges, necessitating continuous adaptation and upgrading of industries.

However, China's capitalist-communist hybrid system has also given rise to income inequality and social disparities. While the economic reforms have lifted millions out of poverty, there remain significant disparities in wealth distribution and access to opportunities. The government's focus on inclusive growth and poverty alleviation remains a pressing challenge.

The sustainability of China's economic model and its implications for future development are subjects of great interest. As China strives to transition towards a more sustainable and consumption-driven economy, it faces the challenges of environmental degradation, resource constraints, and the need for structural reforms. The government's commitment to green development and the promotion of sustainable practices will be crucial in ensuring the long-term viability of China's economic model.

In conclusion, industrialization and urbanization have been the engines driving China's economic expansion. Market-oriented reforms, foreign investments, Special Economic Zones, state-owned enterprise integration, entrepreneurship, private sector development, innovation, technological advancements, globalization, income inequality, social disparities, and sustainability are all intertwined aspects of China's economic success. Understanding the complexities and nuances of these factors is key to comprehending the remarkable journey of the China Economic Experiment and its implications for the global economy.

# Chapter 3: The Role of Foreign Investments in China's Economic Transformation

Attracting Foreign Direct Investment (FDI)

Foreign Direct Investment (FDI) has played a crucial role in the remarkable success story of China's economic experiment. This subchapter explores the various strategies and initiatives employed by the Chinese government to attract FDI, and the significant impact it has had on China's economic transformation.

China's transition from a planned to a market economy was marked by a deliberate focus on attracting FDI. The government recognized the need for foreign capital, technology, and expertise to drive economic growth and development. To facilitate this, China established Special Economic Zones (SEZs) in the late 1970s, offering preferential policies and incentives to foreign investors. These SEZs served as experimental grounds for market-oriented reforms and became magnets for FDI.

The success of SEZs in attracting FDI led to the expansion of similar zones across the country, creating a favorable investment climate. The Chinese government implemented policies to streamline administrative procedures, reduce bureaucratic hurdles, and provide a more level playing field for foreign investors. These efforts helped create a business-friendly environment, fostering a surge in FDI inflows.

Another key factor in attracting FDI was the integration of state-owned enterprises (SOEs) into a capitalist economic system. The Chinese government introduced reforms to make SOEs more market-oriented and opened up sectors previously restricted to private enterprises. This move not only increased competition but also made

China more attractive to foreign investors, who saw opportunities for partnership and collaboration with SOEs.

Furthermore, the development of entrepreneurship and the private sector played a vital role in attracting FDI. The government encouraged the growth of small and medium-sized enterprises (SMEs), providing them with financial support and favorable policies. These dynamic and innovative enterprises became attractive partners for foreign investors, leading to increased FDI inflows.

China's commitment to innovation and technological advancements also played a significant role in attracting FDI. The government invested heavily in research and development, promoting a culture of innovation and intellectual property protection. This created an environment conducive to foreign investors looking to tap into China's technological capabilities and market potential.

The impact of globalization on China's economic experiment cannot be understated. China's integration into the global economy through trade liberalization and the establishment of global supply chains attracted FDI from multinational corporations seeking access to China's vast consumer market and competitive manufacturing capabilities.

However, China's economic success has not been without challenges. Income inequality and social disparities have emerged as significant concerns in its capitalist-communist hybrid system. The government is now focusing on addressing these issues through social welfare programs and inclusive economic policies.

The sustainability of China's economic model and its implications for future development is a topic of ongoing debate. As China continues to evolve and adapt, the government is striving to strike a balance between economic growth, environmental sustainability, and social stability.

In conclusion, China's success in attracting FDI has been instrumental in its economic transformation. Through the establishment of SEZs, integration of SOEs, development of entrepreneurship, and commitment to innovation, China has created an attractive investment climate. However, challenges such as income inequality and sustainability need to be addressed for future development. The Chinese economic experiment continues to be a subject of interest for economists, politicians, diplomats, scholars, and those interested in the successes, challenges, and opportunities of using a capitalist economic system in a communist regime.

Joint Ventures and Technology Transfer

China's economic transformation into a capitalist economy while maintaining its communist regime has been a remarkable success story. One of the key drivers of this success has been the strategic use of joint ventures and technology transfer.

Joint ventures have played a crucial role in China's economic experiment by attracting foreign investments and facilitating the transfer of technology and knowledge. Through joint ventures, foreign companies have been able to enter the Chinese market and tap into its vast consumer base. At the same time, Chinese firms have gained access to advanced technologies, managerial expertise, and global markets.

The impact of market-oriented reforms on China's economic growth has been significant, and joint ventures have been instrumental in driving this growth. By partnering with foreign companies, Chinese firms have been able to learn best practices, improve their production processes, and enhance their competitiveness. This has led to a rapid increase in productivity and efficiency, fueling China's economic expansion.

Special Economic Zones (SEZs) have played a crucial role in attracting foreign investments and promoting technology transfer. These designated areas offer preferential policies and incentives to foreign investors, encouraging them to set up joint ventures with Chinese partners. SEZs have been instrumental in creating a conducive environment for technology transfer, fostering innovation, and catalyzing economic development.

The integration of state-owned enterprises (SOEs) into a capitalist economic system has also been facilitated through joint ventures. By partnering with private and foreign companies, SOEs have been able to improve their efficiency, enhance their competitiveness, and adapt to market-oriented reforms. Joint ventures have provided the necessary impetus for SOEs to embrace market forces and become more dynamic players in the Chinese economy.

The development of entrepreneurship and the private sector have been key drivers of China's economic success. Joint ventures have played a crucial role in nurturing entrepreneurship by providing access to capital, technology, and markets. They have also enabled the transfer of entrepreneurial skills and knowledge, promoting the growth of domestic businesses and the emergence of a vibrant private sector.

However, the transition from a planned to a market economy has not been without challenges. The influx of foreign investments and technology has led to income inequality and social disparities. While the coastal regions have experienced rapid economic growth, the inland regions have lagged behind. Addressing these regional disparities and ensuring inclusive growth remain key challenges for China's economic experiment.

Innovation and technological advancements have been central to China's economic achievements. Joint ventures have facilitated the transfer of advanced technologies, fostering innovation and enabling

Chinese firms to compete globally. The Chinese government has also encouraged indigenous innovation through policies such as intellectual property protection and research and development incentives.

Globalization has played a significant role in China's economic experiment. Joint ventures have facilitated the integration of the Chinese economy into global supply chains, enabling China to become the world's manufacturing hub. However, the ongoing trade tensions and protectionist measures pose challenges to China's economic model, and the country needs to navigate these challenges to sustain its economic growth.

The sustainability of China's economic model and its implications for future development remain a subject of debate. While China has achieved remarkable economic success, it faces challenges such as environmental degradation, demographic changes, and an aging population. The Chinese government needs to address these challenges and transition towards a more sustainable and inclusive economic model to ensure long-term development.

In conclusion, joint ventures and technology transfer have been instrumental in driving China's economic experiment. They have facilitated foreign investments, promoted technology transfer, and fostered innovation. However, challenges such as income inequality, regional disparities, and environmental degradation need to be addressed to ensure the sustainability of China's economic model and its implications for future development.

China's Integration into Global Supply Chains

China's integration into global supply chains has been a central factor in its economic transformation and remarkable growth over the past few decades. This subchapter explores the various aspects and implications of China's integration into global supply chains, shedding light on the factors that have contributed to its success and the challenges it faces.

China's economic experiment, utilizing a capitalist economic system in a communist regime, has yielded significant successes. One of the key drivers of this success has been China's ability to attract foreign investments. Market-oriented reforms have played a crucial role in opening up the Chinese economy to foreign investments and encouraging the inflow of capital, technology, and expertise. This has facilitated the integration of China into global supply chains, allowing it to become a major player in the global economy.

Special Economic Zones (SEZs) have been instrumental in China's economic success. These designated areas have offered favorable conditions for foreign investments, including tax incentives, streamlined regulations, and infrastructure development. SEZs have acted as catalysts for economic growth, attracting multinational corporations and enabling the transfer of technology and knowledge.

The integration of state-owned enterprises (SOEs) into a capitalist economic system has also been a crucial element of China's economic transformation. Through market-oriented reforms, many SOEs have transitioned into competitive entities, contributing to the efficiency and productivity of the Chinese economy.

China's economic experiment has fostered the development of entrepreneurship and the private sector. The government's support for private enterprise and the relaxation of regulations have encouraged innovation, investment, and job creation. This has led to the emergence of a dynamic and vibrant private sector, which has significantly contributed to China's economic growth.

While China's transition from a planned to a market economy has presented numerous opportunities, it has also posed challenges. The shift has brought about income inequality and social disparities, with certain segments of society benefiting more than others. Addressing these disparities and ensuring a more inclusive growth model remains a crucial task for China's policymakers.

Innovation and technological advancements have played a pivotal role in China's economic achievements. The government's focus on research and development, coupled with its investment in science and technology, has enabled China to become a global leader in areas such as artificial intelligence, renewable energy, and e-commerce.

The impact of globalization on China's economic experiment cannot be understated. China's integration into global supply chains has allowed it to become the world's factory, benefiting from economies of scale and access to global markets. However, globalization has also exposed China to external risks and vulnerabilities, as evidenced by the recent trade tensions with the United States.

The sustainability of China's economic model and its implications for future development is a subject of much debate. As China continues to grow and evolve, it must address environmental challenges, such as pollution and resource depletion, while also ensuring social stability and inclusive growth.

In conclusion, China's integration into global supply chains has been a key driver of its economic success. By attracting foreign investments, developing special economic zones, transforming state-owned enterprises, fostering entrepreneurship, promoting innovation, and embracing globalization, China has positioned itself as a major player in the global economy. However, it must navigate the challenges and ensure the sustainability of its economic model to secure future development.

The Benefits and Challenges of Foreign Investments

Foreign investments have played a crucial role in the success story of China's economic experiment. As the country transitioned from a planned to a market economy, the inflow of foreign capital and expertise has been instrumental in driving economic growth and transforming China into the economic powerhouse it is today. However, foreign investments have also presented certain challenges that the Chinese government has had to navigate.

One of the key benefits of foreign investments is the transfer of technology and know-how. Multinational corporations bring with them advanced technologies, management practices, and innovative ideas that can significantly enhance the productivity and competitiveness of domestic industries. This transfer of knowledge has been particularly evident in Special Economic Zones (SEZs), which have attracted a large share of foreign investments. These zones, characterized by preferential policies and incentives for foreign investors, have served as testing grounds for market-oriented reforms and have played a crucial role in China's economic success.

Foreign investments have also provided a much-needed injection of capital into China's economy. Through joint ventures, strategic partnerships, and direct investments, foreign companies have contributed to the development of infrastructure, manufacturing facilities, and other critical sectors. This influx of capital has not only created jobs but has also stimulated domestic demand and consumption, driving economic growth.

However, foreign investments have come with their fair share of challenges. One of the main concerns is the potential for over-reliance on foreign capital and technology. As China integrates into the global economy, it must ensure that it maintains control over its economic destiny and does not become overly dependent on external forces. This requires striking a balance between attracting foreign investments and protecting domestic industries.

Another challenge is the issue of income inequality and social disparities. While foreign investments have created jobs and lifted millions out of poverty, they have also contributed to a widening wealth gap. The Chinese government must address this issue to ensure that the benefits of economic growth are shared more equitably among its citizens.

Furthermore, the sustainability of China's economic model is a pressing concern. As the country faces environmental challenges and a need to transition to a more sustainable and inclusive growth path, foreign investments can play a crucial role in promoting green technologies and sustainable development practices.

In conclusion, foreign investments have been instrumental in China's economic transformation. They have brought in advanced technologies, capital, and expertise, driving economic growth and increasing competitiveness. However, challenges such as over-reliance on foreign capital, income inequality, and sustainability must be addressed to ensure the long-term success of China's economic experiment. The Chinese government must strike a delicate balance between attracting foreign investments and protecting domestic industries, while also promoting inclusive and sustainable development for the benefit of all its citizens.

# Chapter 4: The Influence of Special Economic Zones (SEZs) on China's Economic Success

The Birth and Development of SEZs

Special Economic Zones (SEZs) have played a pivotal role in the success of the China Economic Experiment, serving as catalysts for economic growth and transformation. This subchapter explores the origin, evolution, and impact of SEZs on China's economic development.

The concept of SEZs was first introduced in China in the late 1970s as part of Deng Xiaoping's market-oriented reforms. These designated areas offered preferential policies and incentives to attract foreign investments and promote international trade. The establishment of SEZs marked a departure from China's centrally planned economy and signaled the country's willingness to experiment with capitalist principles within a communist regime.

The first SEZ was established in Shenzhen in 1980, transforming a small fishing village into a global economic powerhouse. The success of Shenzhen as a manufacturing and export base encouraged the government to replicate the model in other regions, leading to the establishment of SEZs in cities such as Shanghai, Guangzhou, and Xiamen. These zones served as laboratories for testing market-oriented policies, including relaxed regulations, tax incentives, and streamlined bureaucratic processes.

Foreign investments played a crucial role in the development of SEZs and the overall economic transformation of China. Multinational corporations were attracted by the abundant labor force, low production costs, and access to a vast consumer market. The influx of foreign capital brought advanced technologies, management expertise, and international connections, propelling China's industrialization and export-oriented growth.

The success of SEZs extended beyond attracting foreign investments. They also served as incubators for entrepreneurship and the development of the private sector. The relaxed regulations and supportive environment within SEZs allowed domestic businesses to flourish, contributing to job creation, innovation, and wealth generation. By nurturing a dynamic private sector alongside state-owned enterprises (SOEs), China was able to harness the benefits of both systems and leverage its resources effectively.

The development of SEZs was not without challenges. As China transitioned from a planned to a market economy, it faced the task of balancing economic liberalization with social stability. Income inequality and social disparities emerged as significant issues, with wealth concentrated in the coastal regions where the SEZs were located. The government had to implement policies to address these disparities and ensure inclusive growth and social cohesion.

Despite these challenges, SEZs have been instrumental in China's economic achievements. They have facilitated the integration of China into the global economy, stimulated technological advancements and innovation, and contributed to the country's high economic growth rates. The sustainability of China's economic model, with SEZs at its core, will undoubtedly shape the country's future development and have implications for the global economic landscape.

SEZs as Laboratories for Economic Experimentation

Special Economic Zones (SEZs) have played a crucial role in China's economic success story, serving as laboratories for economic experimentation. These designated areas have provided a testing ground for market-oriented reforms, attracting foreign investments, and fostering the development of entrepreneurship and the private sector.

In the early stages of China's economic transformation, the government recognized the need for experimental zones to test and implement new economic policies. SEZs, such as Shenzhen and Xiamen, were established in the late 1970s and early 1980s to serve as pilot areas for market-oriented reforms. These zones were granted more autonomy and flexibility in terms of economic policies, allowing them to operate under a different set of rules compared to the rest of the country.

The success of SEZs in attracting foreign investments and promoting economic growth has been remarkable. These zones offered various incentives to foreign investors, including tax breaks, streamlined administrative procedures, and access to a well-trained labor force. As a result, numerous multinational corporations set up operations within SEZs, contributing to China's economic transformation.

Moreover, SEZs played a significant role in integrating state-owned enterprises (SOEs) into a capitalist economic system. By allowing SOEs to operate alongside private enterprises within the same zones, the government aimed to enhance their efficiency and competitiveness. This move facilitated the gradual transition of these enterprises towards a market-oriented approach, improving their performance and contributing to China's economic growth.

SEZs also acted as breeding grounds for entrepreneurship and the development of the private sector. These zones provided a conducive environment for individuals to start their businesses, with fewer bureaucratic hurdles and more favorable regulations. The success stories of entrepreneurs within SEZs inspired others to follow suit, leading to the rapid expansion of the private sector in China's economy.

However, the path to success has not been without challenges. The transition from a planned to a market economy has posed significant hurdles, including income inequality and social disparities. While economic growth has lifted millions out of poverty, it has also created a wealth gap, with some regions and social groups benefiting more than others. Balancing the need for economic development with social equity remains a constant challenge for China's policymakers.

Furthermore, the sustainability of China's economic model and its implications for future development is a topic of great importance. As China continues to rely heavily on exports and foreign investments, it must navigate the challenges posed by globalization and evolving global economic dynamics. The country's ability to foster innovation and technological advancements will be crucial in maintaining its competitive edge and sustaining long-term growth.

In conclusion, SEZs have served as vital laboratories for economic experimentation in China. These zones have played a pivotal role in attracting foreign investments, integrating state-owned enterprises into a capitalist economic system, and fostering entrepreneurship and the private sector. While facing challenges such as income inequality and the need for sustainable development, China's economic experiment has demonstrated the benefits of using a capitalist economic system within a communist regime. The success of SEZs has not only transformed China's economy but also provided valuable lessons for economists, politicians, diplomats, and scholars worldwide.

Lessons Learned from SEZs: Replication and Expansion

Special Economic Zones (SEZs) have played a crucial role in China's economic transformation and have been instrumental in its success story of capitalism in a communist regime. These designated areas have provided valuable lessons that can be replicated and expanded upon to further drive economic growth and development in China. In this subchapter, we explore the key lessons learned from SEZs and their implications for economists, politicians, diplomats, and scholars.

One of the first lessons learned is the importance of creating a conducive environment for foreign investments. SEZs have attracted significant foreign direct investments (FDIs), which have been instrumental in driving China's economic growth. Policymakers should focus on providing attractive incentives, such as tax breaks, streamlined bureaucracy, and improved infrastructure, to encourage more FDIs and replicate the success seen in SEZs.

Another lesson learned is the need to integrate state-owned enterprises (SOEs) into a capitalist economic system. SEZs have successfully demonstrated how SOEs can adapt and thrive in a market-oriented environment. This lesson is particularly relevant as China continues its transition from a planned to a market economy. Policymakers should focus on implementing reforms that enable SOEs to operate in a competitive market, fostering innovation, efficiency, and profitability.

SEZs have also played a vital role in fostering entrepreneurship and the growth of the private sector. Lessons from these zones highlight the importance of nurturing a favorable ecosystem for startups and small and medium-sized enterprises (SMEs) to flourish. Policymakers should focus on providing access to capital, reducing bureaucratic hurdles, and fostering innovation to encourage entrepreneurship and further develop the private sector.

Furthermore, SEZs have showcased the significance of innovation and technological advancements in China's economic achievements. Lessons learned emphasize the need for continuous investment in research and development, promoting collaboration between academia and industry, and fostering an environment that encourages technological advancements.

Finally, the sustainability of China's economic model and its implications for future development is a crucial lesson derived from SEZs. Policymakers must carefully balance economic growth with social and environmental considerations. They should focus on addressing income inequality and social disparities, promoting inclusive growth, and ensuring sustainable development for the long term.

In conclusion, the lessons learned from SEZs provide valuable insights for economists, politicians, diplomats, and scholars. Replicating and expanding upon these lessons can further drive China's economic growth and development. By attracting foreign investments, integrating SOEs into a market-oriented system, fostering entrepreneurship and innovation, and promoting sustainable development, China can continue its successful economic experiment and serve as a model for other economies around the world.

# Chapter 5: The Integration of State-owned Enterprises (SOEs) into a Capitalist Economic System

The Evolution of SOEs in China

State-owned enterprises (SOEs) have played a crucial role in the economic transformation of China. Their evolution over the years is a testament to the success of the China Economic Experiment, which combines elements of capitalism within a communist regime. This subchapter will delve into the various aspects of SOEs' development and their integration into a capitalist economic system.

SOEs in China have undergone significant changes since the country's economic reforms began in the late 1970s. Initially, these enterprises operated under a centrally planned economy with limited market-oriented reforms. However, as China embraced market-oriented policies, SOEs gradually shifted their focus towards profitability and efficiency.

One of the key factors that influenced the evolution of SOEs in China was the role of foreign investments. Foreign direct investment (FDI) played a crucial role in improving the efficiency and competitiveness of Chinese SOEs. By partnering with foreign companies, SOEs were able to access advanced technology, management expertise, and global markets. This led to an overall improvement in their performance and contributed to China's economic growth.

Furthermore, the establishment of Special Economic Zones (SEZs) played a pivotal role in the success of SOEs. These zones provided a favorable environment for experimentation and innovation, allowing SOEs to adapt to market-oriented reforms more effectively. The SEZs' flexible policies, such as tax incentives and streamlined regulations, attracted both domestic and foreign investments, which further enhanced the performance of SOEs.

The integration of SOEs into a capitalist economic system also led to the development of entrepreneurship and the private sector in China. As market-oriented reforms took hold, private enterprises emerged, competing with SOEs and driving economic growth. This shift created a dynamic business environment, fostering innovation, and increasing employment opportunities.

However, the transition from a planned to a market economy came with its own set of challenges and opportunities. SOEs faced the challenge of adapting to market forces, restructuring, and improving their efficiency. Moreover, the issue of income inequality and social disparities arose as a result of the simultaneous existence of a capitalist-communist hybrid system.

Innovation and technological advancements have also played a crucial role in China's economic achievements. SOEs have embraced innovation to improve their productivity, competitiveness, and sustainability. The Chinese government's focus on research and development has further contributed to the technological advancements of SOEs, which has been instrumental in their success.

Globalization has been another significant factor in China's economic experiment. SOEs have expanded their presence in global markets, transforming China into a major global economic player. This has further propelled the country's economic growth and development.

The sustainability of China's economic model and its implications for future development remain a topic of debate. While SOEs have made significant contributions to China's economic success, there are concerns about their efficiency, transparency, and accountability.

Balancing the role of SOEs with the growth of the private sector will be critical for ensuring sustainable economic development in China.

In conclusion, the evolution of SOEs in China is a testament to the success of the China Economic Experiment. Their integration into a capitalist economic system, driven by market-oriented reforms, foreign investments, and technological advancements, has propelled China's economic growth. However, challenges such as income inequality and the need for sustainability remain, and policymakers must address these issues to ensure continued economic success.

Restructuring and Privatization of SOEs

Restructuring and Privatization of SOEs: Transitioning China's State-Owned Enterprises into a Market Economy

The restructuring and privatization of State-Owned Enterprises (SOEs) has played a crucial role in China's economic transformation and its success story of implementing a capitalist economic system within a communist regime. This subchapter explores the significant impact of market-oriented reforms on China's economic growth, the challenges and opportunities of transitioning SOEs into a capitalist economic system, and the sustainability of China's economic model.

China's journey towards economic success began with market-oriented reforms that aimed to enhance efficiency, productivity, and competitiveness. The restructuring of SOEs was a key element of these reforms. By introducing market principles, such as competition and profit incentives, China aimed to transform its bloated and inefficient SOEs into dynamic and market-driven entities. This process involved restructuring and privatization, which allowed for greater flexibility, innovation, and accountability.

The integration of SOEs into a capitalist economic system has brought about numerous benefits. Privatization has led to increased competition, improved efficiency, and enhanced productivity. With private ownership, SOEs have become more responsive to market demands, resulting in better allocation of resources. Moreover, the influx of private capital and foreign investments has injected much-needed funds and expertise into these enterprises, further accelerating their growth and development.

The development of entrepreneurship and the private sector has been a crucial component of China's economic success. As SOEs were restructured and privatized, it created opportunities for the emergence of a vibrant private sector. The government's supportive policies and initiatives have fostered a conducive environment for entrepreneurship, leading to the rise of innovative and dynamic enterprises. These private enterprises have played a significant role in driving economic growth, job creation, and technological advancements.

However, the transition from a planned to a market economy has not been without challenges. The process of restructuring and privatization has faced resistance from vested interests and encountered obstacles such as overcapacity, layoffs, and social unrest. Furthermore, income inequality and social disparities have emerged as pressing issues within China's capitalist-communist hybrid system. Addressing these challenges requires a comprehensive approach that ensures inclusive growth, social protection, and equitable opportunities for all.

Looking ahead, the sustainability of China's economic model and its implications for future development are critical considerations. As China continues to navigate the complexities of a globalized world, it must strike a balance between economic growth, social stability, and environmental sustainability. Embracing innovation, technological advancements, and sustainable practices will be vital in maintaining China's economic momentum and achieving long-term prosperity.

In conclusion, the restructuring and privatization of SOEs have been instrumental in China's economic success story. The integration of market-oriented reforms, foreign investments, and the development of a vibrant private sector have propelled China's growth and transformation. However, challenges remain, particularly in addressing income inequality and ensuring the sustainability of China's economic model. By learning from its experiences and embracing innovation, China can continue to evolve and adapt, paving the way for future development and prosperity.

The Role of SOEs in China's Economic Development

State-owned enterprises (SOEs) have played a significant role in China's economic development, contributing to the country's remarkable transformation from a planned to a market economy. This subchapter examines how SOEs have integrated into a capitalist economic system and explores their impact on China's economic achievements.

SOEs have been a key instrument used by the Chinese government to implement its economic policies and achieve its development goals. These enterprises have been involved in various sectors, including energy, telecommunications, banking, and infrastructure. Through their strategic investments and operations, SOEs have helped stimulate economic growth, create employment opportunities, and drive technological advancements.

One of the notable successes of China's economic experiment is the effective utilization of SOEs as engines of economic growth. The government's control over these enterprises has allowed for strategic planning and targeted investments in priority sectors. This has enabled the country to rapidly develop critical infrastructure, such as roads, railways, and airports, which has facilitated trade and economic integration.

Furthermore, SOEs have played a crucial role in promoting innovation and technological advancements in China. By investing in research and development, these enterprises have contributed to the country's rise as a global technological powerhouse. Their financial resources and access to government support have allowed them to invest in cutting-edge technologies, such as artificial intelligence, renewable energy, and biotechnology.

The integration of SOEs into a capitalist economic system has also created opportunities for entrepreneurship and the growth of the private sector. As the Chinese government gradually embraced market-oriented reforms, it began to encourage private enterprises to compete with SOEs in various sectors. This competition has fueled innovation, improved efficiency, and enhanced consumer choice.

However, the role of SOEs in China's economic development has not been without challenges. The dominance of these enterprises in certain sectors has led to concerns about market monopolies and unfair competition. Additionally, the inefficiencies and lack of transparency associated with some SOEs have hindered their ability to adapt to market forces effectively.

Looking towards the future, the sustainability of China's economic model and the role of SOEs will be critical. As the country faces increasing pressure to address income inequality and social disparities, the Chinese government will need to strike a balance between promoting market competition and ensuring the welfare of its citizens.

In conclusion, the role of SOEs in China's economic development has been significant. These enterprises have contributed to the country's economic growth, stimulated innovation, and facilitated the integration of China into the global economy. However, their dominance and inefficiencies present challenges that need to be addressed for sustainable and inclusive development.

## Balancing State Control and Market Efficiency

In the fascinating journey of the China economic experiment, one of the key challenges has been finding the optimal balance between state control and market efficiency. This delicate equilibrium has been crucial in enabling the Chinese economy to flourish under a unique capitalist economic system within a communist regime. In this subchapter, we will explore the strategies and policies that have contributed to this successful balancing act.

China's economic transformation has been driven by market-oriented reforms that have unleashed the potential of its vast population and abundant resources. These reforms have fostered an environment conducive to economic growth by encouraging entrepreneurship, attracting foreign investments, and establishing Special Economic Zones (SEZs). The impact of market-oriented reforms on China's economic growth has been nothing short of remarkable, propelling the nation to become the world's second-largest economy.

Foreign investments have played a pivotal role in China's economic transformation. They have not only provided capital and advanced technologies but also facilitated knowledge transfers and market access. The integration of state-owned enterprises (SOEs) into a capitalist economic system has also been instrumental in China's economic success. By subjecting these enterprises to market competition and promoting efficiency and innovation, the Chinese government has harnessed the potential of SOEs while maintaining control over key sectors of the economy.

The development of entrepreneurship and the private sector has been another crucial factor in China's economic achievements. The government's embrace of private enterprises has created an environment that encourages innovation, fosters competition, and drives economic growth. This has led to the emergence of a vibrant private sector that complements the state-owned enterprises, contributing significantly to China's economic success.

However, this transition from a planned to a market economy has not been without its challenges. China has had to grapple with income inequality and social disparities resulting from rapid economic growth. The government has recognized these challenges and has implemented measures to address them, including poverty alleviation programs and initiatives to promote inclusive growth.

The sustainability of China's economic model and its implications for future development are also important considerations. As China continues to navigate its economic experiment, it must be mindful of the impact of globalization and technological advancements. Embracing innovation and technological advancements will be crucial in driving future economic growth and maintaining China's competitive edge in the global economy.

In conclusion, the successful balancing of state control and market efficiency has been a key driver of China's economic experiment. By implementing market-oriented reforms, attracting foreign investments, integrating state-owned enterprises, and promoting entrepreneurship and private sector development, China has achieved remarkable economic growth. However, challenges such as income inequality and the sustainability of the economic model must be carefully addressed to ensure a prosperous future for China's economy.

# Chapter 6: The Development of Entrepreneurship and the Private Sector in China's Economy

The Rise of Private Enterprises

In "The China Economic Experiment: A Success Story of Capitalism in a Communist Regime," this subchapter explores the remarkable rise of private enterprises in China and its significant implications for the country's economic transformation. This section addresses economists, politicians, diplomats, scholars, and those interested in the various aspects of China's unique economic experiment.

China's adoption of a capitalist economic system within a communist dictatorship has led to unprecedented successes. One of the key drivers behind this achievement has been the rise of private enterprises. Initially, the Chinese government introduced market-oriented reforms in the late 1970s, which gradually allowed for the emergence of private businesses. These reforms proved instrumental in propelling China's economic growth to new heights.

Foreign investments have played a crucial role in China's economic transformation. As the country opened up to the global market, foreign investors poured capital into various sectors, contributing to job creation, technology transfer, and infrastructure development. This influx of foreign investments has been particularly influential in the Special Economic Zones (SEZs), which have served as experimental grounds for market-oriented policies and have attracted both domestic and foreign entrepreneurs.

The integration of state-owned enterprises (SOEs) into a capitalist economic system has presented a unique challenge for China. While these SOEs have traditionally dominated various sectors, their transition into a market economy required substantial reforms. The government has gradually introduced measures to increase efficiency, encourage competition, and reduce bureaucratic red tape, allowing for fair competition between SOEs and private enterprises.

China's economic success has also been driven by the development of entrepreneurship and the private sector. The government has actively supported the growth of small and medium-sized enterprises (SMEs), recognizing their potential as drivers of innovation, employment, and economic diversification. This focus on entrepreneurship has created a vibrant ecosystem that fosters innovation and contributes to China's economic achievements.

However, China's transition from a planned to a market economy has not been without challenges. Income inequality and social disparities have emerged as pressing issues in this capitalist-communist hybrid system. The government has taken steps to address these concerns, implementing policies to reduce inequality and improve social welfare programs. Nevertheless, sustaining the momentum of China's economic model remains a critical task for future development.

China's economic experiment has been greatly influenced by globalization. The country's integration into the global market has not only facilitated trade and investment but also exposed China to international competition. To maintain its economic growth, China has continuously emphasized the importance of innovation and technological advancements, allowing the country to enhance its competitiveness on a global scale.

In conclusion, the rise of private enterprises has played a pivotal role in China's economic success. Through market-oriented reforms, the integration of state-owned enterprises, and the development of entrepreneurship, China has been able to leverage the benefits of capitalism within a communist regime. However, challenges such as income inequality and sustainability remain, requiring continued efforts to ensure the future prosperity of China's economic model.

Government Support for Entrepreneurship

One of the key factors contributing to the success of the China Economic Experiment is the government's unwavering support for entrepreneurship. Despite being a communist regime, the Chinese government has recognized the importance of fostering a vibrant private sector and encouraging entrepreneurial activities as drivers of economic growth and development.

The government has implemented various policies and initiatives to promote entrepreneurship and support the growth of small and medium-sized enterprises (SMEs). One such initiative is the establishment of Special Economic Zones (SEZs), which provide a favorable business environment for both domestic and foreign entrepreneurs. These SEZs offer tax incentives, streamlined regulations, and access to infrastructure, attracting both local and international investors.

Moreover, the government has actively encouraged innovation and technological advancements through targeted policies and funding. It has established numerous research and development centers and technology parks to support entrepreneurs in developing cutting-edge technologies and products. Additionally, the government has implemented policies to protect intellectual property rights, which are crucial for fostering innovation and encouraging entrepreneurship.

In terms of financing, the government has set up various funds and programs to provide financial support to entrepreneurs. For instance, it has established the National SME Development Fund, which offers loans and subsidies to small businesses. Additionally, the government has encouraged the establishment of venture capital firms and angel investor networks to provide funding for start-ups and innovative projects.

Furthermore, the Chinese government has played a crucial role in integrating state-owned enterprises (SOEs) into a capitalist economic system. It has implemented reforms to transform these traditionally inefficient and bureaucratic entities into more market-oriented and competitive entities. This has created opportunities for entrepreneurs to collaborate with SOEs, allowing for the transfer of technology and expertise.

However, China's transition from a planned to a market economy has also presented challenges. One of the major challenges is the issue of income inequality and social disparities. While the economic reforms have lifted millions out of poverty, income inequality has also widened, leading to social tensions. The government has recognized this issue and has implemented policies to address the wealth gap and promote inclusive growth.

In conclusion, the Chinese government's support for entrepreneurship has been instrumental in the success of the China Economic Experiment. Through the establishment of SEZs, support for innovation, access to financing, and the integration of SOEs into a capitalist economic system, the government has created a conducive environment for entrepreneurs to thrive. However, challenges such as income inequality and sustainability need to be addressed to ensure the long-term success of China's economic model.

Challenges and Opportunities for Small and Medium-sized Enterprises (SMEs)

Small and Medium-sized Enterprises (SMEs) have played a crucial role in the success story of China's economic experiment. As the country transitioned from a planned to a market economy, SMEs emerged as key drivers of growth, innovation, and job creation. However, they also face a unique set of challenges and opportunities that shape their role in China's capitalist-communist hybrid system.

One of the major challenges for SMEs in China is the competition from state-owned enterprises (SOEs). These SOEs have traditionally enjoyed preferential treatment and access to resources, giving them a competitive edge over their smaller counterparts. This creates an uneven playing field and hinders the growth and development of SMEs. Addressing this issue requires the implementation of policies that promote fair competition and create a level playing field for all businesses.

Another challenge for SMEs is accessing financing. Despite efforts to improve access to credit, SMEs still face difficulties in obtaining loans from traditional financial institutions. This hampers their ability to invest in research and development, expand their operations, and innovate. To address this, the government needs to further enhance financial support mechanisms specifically tailored to the needs of SMEs, such as establishing specialized banks or providing tax incentives for investors in this sector.

However, despite these challenges, SMEs also have significant opportunities in China's economic experiment. The government has recognized the importance of SMEs in driving innovation and economic growth, and has implemented policies to foster their development. These include tax incentives, simplified administrative procedures, and increased support for research and development activities. SMEs can leverage these opportunities to tap into the vast consumer market and contribute to China's economic transformation.

Moreover, the rise of e-commerce and digital platforms has opened new avenues for SMEs to reach customers both domestically and globally. Online marketplaces provide a cost-effective way for SMEs to showcase their products and expand their reach. This digital revolution has the potential to level the playing field for SMEs and empower them to compete with larger enterprises.

In conclusion, while SMEs in China face significant challenges, they also have ample opportunities to thrive and contribute to the country's economic success. By addressing the barriers they face, such as unfair competition and limited access to financing, and leveraging the opportunities presented by digitalization and government support, SMEs can continue to drive innovation, create jobs, and play a crucial role in China's economic experiment.

The Role of Innovation and Technology in Private Sector Growth

In the quest to understand the remarkable success of the China Economic Experiment, it is impossible to overlook the pivotal role played by innovation and technology in driving private sector growth. This subchapter will delve into the ways in which China's relentless focus on innovation and technological advancements has propelled its economy to unprecedented heights, captivating economists, politicians, diplomats, and scholars alike.

China's economic transformation has been built on a foundation of market-oriented reforms, which have facilitated the integration of private enterprises into the once solely state-dominated economy. However, it is the infusion of innovation and technology that has truly propelled the private sector to unimaginable heights. Through strategic investments in research and development, China has nurtured a culture of innovation that has enabled its companies to compete on a global scale.

One of the key factors driving China's economic success is the establishment of Special Economic Zones (SEZs). These zones serve as incubators for innovation, attracting both domestic and foreign investments. By providing a conducive environment for cutting-edge research and development, SEZs have fostered a spirit of entrepreneurship and creativity, fueling the growth of the private sector.

Moreover, the integration of state-owned enterprises (SOEs) into a capitalist economic system has been instrumental in leveraging innovation and technology for private sector growth. By introducing market-oriented reforms within these enterprises, China has created an ecosystem that encourages technological advancements and rewards innovative ideas. This not only enhances the competitiveness of these enterprises but also stimulates the overall private sector growth.

China's transition from a planned to a market economy has presented both challenges and opportunities. However, it is through embracing innovation and technology that China has been able to harness the potential of this transition. Technological advancements have allowed China to leapfrog traditional stages of development, paving the way for rapid economic growth.

The impact of globalization on China's economic experiment cannot be understated. By embracing global trade and investment, China has been able to access cutting-edge technologies and knowledge, fostering innovation and driving private sector growth. Globalization has also opened up new markets for Chinese companies, fueling their expansion and contributing to overall economic prosperity.

However, it is important to acknowledge that China's economic model has not been without its flaws. Income inequality and social disparities persist within the capitalist-communist hybrid system, posing challenges to sustainable development. Ensuring the sustainability of China's economic model will require addressing these disparities and creating an inclusive environment that allows all segments of society to benefit from economic growth.

In conclusion, innovation and technology have been the driving forces behind the private sector growth in China's economic experiment. Through a commitment to research and development, the establishment of Special Economic Zones, and the integration of state-owned enterprises, China has created an ecosystem that fosters innovation and rewards technological advancements. This, coupled with the impact of globalization, has propelled China's economy to unprecedented levels of success. However, it is important to address income inequality and social disparities to ensure the sustainability of this economic model and pave the way for future development.

# Chapter 7: The Challenges and Opportunities of China's Transition from a Planned to a Market Economy

Overcoming Economic Inefficiencies and Distortions

The China Economic Experiment: A Success Story of Capitalism in a Communist Regime

# Introduction

As economists, politicians, diplomats, and scholars, we gather here today to discuss the remarkable success story of the China Economic Experiment. This subchapter aims to shed light on how China has managed to overcome economic inefficiencies and distortions, paving the way for its transformation into a global economic powerhouse.

Market-oriented Reforms and Economic Growth

China's adoption of market-oriented reforms has played a pivotal role in its economic growth. By gradually embracing capitalist principles, the country has witnessed a surge in productivity, investment, and innovation. These reforms have streamlined bureaucratic processes, eliminated market distortions, and allowed for the efficient allocation of resources.

Foreign Investments and Economic Transformation

Foreign investments have played a crucial role in China's economic transformation. The opening up of the Chinese market to foreign businesses has not only attracted capital but has also brought in advanced technology, managerial expertise, and access to international markets. This inflow of foreign investments has propelled China's economic development and enhanced its competitiveness on a global scale.

The Influence of Special Economic Zones (SEZs)

The establishment of Special Economic Zones (SEZs) has been instrumental in China's economic success. These areas, characterized by preferential policies and incentives, have served as experimental grounds for economic reforms. SEZs have acted as catalysts for foreign investments, technological advancements, and export-oriented industries, driving China's economic growth.

Integration of State-Owned Enterprises (SOEs) into a Capitalist System

China's successful integration of state-owned enterprises (SOEs) into a capitalist economic system has been a key driver of its economic success. These enterprises have undergone significant reforms, including corporatization, market-oriented management, and improved efficiency. This integration has not only increased productivity but has also attracted private investments, fostering healthy competition and innovation.

Development of Entrepreneurship and the Private Sector

The development of entrepreneurship and the private sector in China's economy has been a game-changer. The government's encouragement of private enterprise, coupled with favorable policies, has created a vibrant entrepreneurial ecosystem. This has led to the emergence of numerous innovative startups and a flourishing private sector, contributing significantly to China's economic growth.

Challenges and Opportunities in Transitioning to a Market Economy

China's transition from a planned to a market economy has presented both challenges and opportunities. While market-oriented reforms have unleashed tremendous potential, they have also led to income inequality and social disparities. Addressing these issues remains a critical task for China's policymakers to ensure inclusive and sustainable growth.

The Role of Innovation and Technological Advancements

China's economic achievements have been propelled by its focus on innovation and technological advancements. Through massive investments in research and development, the country has become a global leader in areas such as artificial intelligence, renewable energy, and telecommunications. This has not only enhanced China's global competitiveness but has also driven its economic growth.

The Impact of Globalization

Globalization has played a significant role in China's economic experiment. By embracing international trade and investment, China has integrated itself into the global economy, becoming a major player in international markets. This has not only provided opportunities for economic growth but has also exposed China to external risks and challenges.

Income Inequality and Social Disparities

China's capitalist-communist hybrid system has led to income inequality and social disparities. While economic reforms have lifted millions out of poverty, the gap between the rich and poor has widened. Addressing income inequality and ensuring social welfare remain key challenges for China's future development.

Sustainability of China's Economic Model and Implications for Future Development

The sustainability of China's economic model and its implications for future development remain subjects of debate. As China continues to grow, it must address environmental challenges, resource constraints, and the need for sustainable development. Balancing economic growth with social and environmental considerations will be crucial for China's long-term prosperity.

Conclusion

In conclusion, China's successful economic experiment, combining capitalist principles with a communist regime, has overcome economic inefficiencies and distortions to achieve remarkable growth. Market-oriented reforms, foreign investments, Special Economic Zones, the integration of state-owned enterprises, entrepreneurship, and technological advancements have all contributed to China's economic success. However, challenges such as income inequality and environmental sustainability must be addressed to ensure a prosperous future for China.

Managing the Social Impacts of Economic Reforms

Introduction:

As China continues to undergo rapid economic reforms, it is essential to address the social impacts that accompany these changes. Managing the social consequences of economic reforms is crucial to ensure the sustainability and long-term success of China's unique capitalist-communist hybrid system. This subchapter will explore the various strategies and policies employed by the Chinese government to mitigate the social impacts of its economic experiment.

Balancing Economic Growth and Social Stability:

One of the key challenges in managing the social impacts of economic reforms is striking a balance between economic growth and social stability. China's government has implemented measures to address income inequality and social disparities, recognizing that a harmonious society is essential for sustained economic development.

Investing in Human Capital:

To mitigate the social impacts of economic reforms, China has focused on investing in human capital. The government has implemented policies to enhance education, improve healthcare, and provide social welfare programs to ensure that citizens benefit from economic growth.

Social Safety Nets and Poverty Alleviation:

China has made significant progress in reducing poverty through targeted poverty alleviation programs. The government has implemented social safety nets, including healthcare coverage, unemployment benefits, and pension schemes, to protect vulnerable populations during economic transitions.

Promoting Inclusive Growth:

To address income inequality, China has focused on promoting inclusive growth by supporting the development of entrepreneurship and the private sector. This has provided opportunities for individuals to participate in the economic growth and share its benefits.

Engaging with Stakeholders:

China recognizes the importance of engaging with various stakeholders, including economists, politicians, diplomats, and scholars, to address the social impacts of economic reforms. Through dialogue and collaboration, the government seeks to understand and respond to the concerns and needs of different groups.

Conclusion:

Managing the social impacts of economic reforms is an ongoing challenge for China. The government's proactive approach in investing in human capital, implementing social safety nets, promoting inclusive growth, and engaging with stakeholders has been instrumental in mitigating the adverse effects of economic transformations. However, as China continues its economic experiment, policymakers must remain vigilant in addressing emerging social issues and ensuring the sustainability of its unique economic model. By managing the social impacts effectively, China can foster a harmonious society and continue its remarkable economic success story.

Ensuring Financial Stability and Managing Risks

One of the key factors that has contributed to the success of the China economic experiment is the ability to ensure financial stability and effectively manage risks. In a country that has transitioned from a planned to a market economy, this has been a critical aspect of sustaining economic growth and development.

China's financial system has undergone significant reforms to align with the requirements of a market-oriented economy. These reforms have included the establishment of a central bank, the People's Bank of China, and the development of a robust regulatory framework. This has helped to ensure stability in the financial sector and mitigate the risks associated with market fluctuations.

Foreign investments have played a crucial role in China's economic transformation. These investments have not only brought in capital and technology but have also contributed to the diversification of the economy. However, managing the risks associated with foreign investments has been a priority. China has implemented various measures, such as strict regulatory controls, to safeguard against potential risks and ensure the stability of the financial system.

Special Economic Zones (SEZs) have been instrumental in China's economic success. These zones, which were established to attract foreign investments and promote exports, have provided a testing ground for market-oriented reforms. By allowing for experimentation with different economic policies, SEZs have helped to identify and manage risks before implementing them on a larger scale.

The integration of state-owned enterprises (SOEs) into a capitalist economic system has been another important aspect of China's economic experiment. While SOEs have traditionally been associated with inefficiency and lack of innovation, the government has taken steps to reform these enterprises and make them more competitive. This has involved injecting market-oriented principles into their operations and subjecting them to greater market discipline.

The development of entrepreneurship and the private sector has been a driving force behind China's economic growth. The government has encouraged the establishment of private businesses, provided access to capital, and created a favorable business environment. This has not only contributed to job creation but has also fostered innovation and competition, further enhancing the stability of the economy.

However, the transition from a planned to a market economy has not been without challenges. China has had to grapple with issues such as income inequality and social disparities. The government has recognized these challenges and has implemented policies to address them, including social welfare programs and initiatives to promote inclusive growth.

Innovation and technological advancements have also played a crucial role in China's economic achievements. The country has made significant investments in research and development, resulting in breakthroughs in various sectors. This has helped to enhance productivity, promote competitiveness, and manage risks associated with technological disruptions.

Globalization has had a profound impact on China's economic experiment. The country has embraced globalization by actively participating in international trade and investment. This has not only provided opportunities for economic growth but has also exposed China to external risks. To manage these risks, the government has implemented measures to ensure the stability of the financial system and safeguard against potential shocks.

The sustainability of China's economic model and its implications for future development are critical considerations. As the country continues to evolve, it must navigate challenges such as environmental sustainability, demographic changes, and shifting global dynamics. To ensure long-term stability, China must continue to adapt its economic model, manage risks effectively, and promote inclusive and sustainable growth.

In conclusion, ensuring financial stability and managing risks have been crucial elements in the success of the China economic experiment. Through financial reforms, prudent management of foreign investments, the establishment of SEZs, integration of SOEs into a capitalist system, and fostering entrepreneurship and innovation, China has been able to navigate the challenges of transitioning from a planned to a market economy. However, ongoing efforts are required to address income inequality, promote sustainable development, and navigate the evolving global landscape. By doing so, China can continue to build on its economic achievements and shape its future success.

Balancing Economic Growth with Environmental Sustainability

In the pursuit of rapid economic growth, China has achieved remarkable success by utilizing a capitalist economic system within a communist regime. This subchapter aims to explore the delicate balance between economic development and environmental sustainability in the context of China's economic experiment.

China's market-oriented reforms have been instrumental in driving its economic growth. However, the rapid industrialization and urbanization that accompanied this growth have also resulted in severe environmental degradation. As economists, politicians, diplomats, and scholars, it is crucial to examine the challenges and opportunities of achieving sustainable development in China.

Foreign investments have played a pivotal role in China's economic transformation. These investments have not only brought capital and technology but also triggered a gradual shift towards environmentally-friendly practices. China's integration into the global economy has incentivized the adoption of greener technologies and higher environmental standards.

Special Economic Zones (SEZs) have been instrumental in China's economic success. These zones have provided a platform for experimentation and innovation, enabling local authorities to implement sustainable practices and policies. By focusing on eco-friendly industries and promoting renewable energy sources, SEZs have shown that economic growth and environmental sustainability can go hand in hand.

The integration of state-owned enterprises (SOEs) into a capitalist economic system has also presented opportunities for environmental sustainability. By subjecting these enterprises to market forces and competition, China has encouraged efficiency and innovation, leading to the adoption of cleaner production methods.

The development of entrepreneurship and the private sector have further contributed to China's economic growth. As the private sector continues to expand, there is an increasing emphasis on sustainable business practices. Entrepreneurs are recognizing the importance of environmental stewardship, leading to the emergence of eco-friendly startups and sustainable innovations.

However, China's transition from a planned to a market economy has presented both challenges and opportunities. The rapid pace of economic development has strained natural resources, increased pollution levels, and exacerbated income inequality. It is crucial for policymakers to address these challenges through effective regulations, incentives for sustainable practices, and investments in green technologies.

Innovation and technological advancements have been key drivers of China's economic achievements. By investing in research and development, China has become a global leader in various sectors, including renewable energy. Continued focus on innovation will be essential to ensure sustainable economic growth and mitigate the environmental impact of development.

Furthermore, globalization has shaped China's economic experiment. Integration into the global market has facilitated technology transfer, increased access to capital, and created opportunities for international cooperation on environmental issues. China's engagement with the international community is crucial for achieving long-term environmental sustainability.

The sustainable development of China's economic model is of paramount importance for its future development. As income inequality and social disparities persist, it is vital to ensure that the benefits of economic growth are shared equitably. A sustainable economic model should prioritize social inclusivity and environmental stewardship, paving the way for a prosperous and environmentally responsible China.

In conclusion, the balancing act between economic growth and environmental sustainability is a critical challenge that China faces in its economic experiment. By leveraging market-oriented reforms, foreign investments, SEZs, private sector development, innovation, and globalization, China has the potential to achieve sustainable economic growth. However, it is imperative for policymakers, economists, politicians, diplomats, and scholars to continue exploring strategies and policies that prioritize environmental protection and social wellbeing, ensuring a sustainable and prosperous future for China.

# Chapter 8: The Role of Innovation and Technological Advancements in China's Economic Achievements

China's Innovation-Driven Development Strategy

China's remarkable economic transformation over the past few decades is largely attributed to its innovation-driven development strategy. In this subchapter, we will delve into the key factors and policies that have propelled China's economic success through innovation and technological advancements.

One of the cornerstones of China's innovation-driven development strategy has been its emphasis on research and development (R&D) investments. In recent years, China has significantly increased its R&D spending, surpassing other major economies. This has allowed the country to foster a conducive environment for innovation, enabling the development of cutting-edge technologies and the creation of high-value industries.

Additionally, China has actively promoted collaboration between industry, academia, and government, creating innovation clusters and technology parks that facilitate knowledge transfer and the commercialization of research findings. Special Economic Zones (SEZs) have played a crucial role in this process, attracting foreign investments and facilitating technology transfer. These zones have acted as test beds for market-oriented reforms and have encouraged the integration of state-owned enterprises (SOEs) into a capitalist economic system.

Foreign investments have been instrumental in China's economic transformation, particularly in terms of technology transfer and knowledge spillovers. China has actively encouraged foreign companies to establish research and development centers in the country, facilitating the transfer of advanced technologies and managerial expertise. This has not only enhanced China's domestic capabilities but has also contributed to its integration into global value chains.

China's commitment to nurturing entrepreneurship and the private sector has also been a significant driver of its innovation-led growth. The government has implemented policies to support the establishment and growth of small and medium-sized enterprises (SMEs), fostering a vibrant entrepreneurial ecosystem. This has resulted in the emergence of numerous innovative startups, particularly in sectors such as e-commerce, fintech, and artificial intelligence.

However, China's transition from a planned to a market economy has not been without challenges. The country continues to grapple with income inequality and social disparities, as its capitalist-communist hybrid system creates disparities both regionally and socially. Addressing these disparities remains a key priority for the government to ensure the sustainability of its economic model and avoid potential social unrest.

Looking ahead, the sustainability of China's economic model will depend on its ability to navigate the complex dynamics of globalization. As China's economy becomes increasingly integrated with the global economy, it faces both opportunities and risks. Balancing the need for openness with the challenges of protecting domestic industries and intellectual property rights will be crucial for China's future development.

In conclusion, China's innovation-driven development strategy has been a critical driver of its economic success. By investing in research and development, promoting collaboration, attracting foreign investments, supporting entrepreneurship, and leveraging technological advancements, China has managed to transform its economy and become a global technological powerhouse. However, challenges such as income inequality and the need to adapt to globalization remain, requiring continued efforts to ensure the sustainability and inclusivity of China's economic model.

The Rise of High-Tech Industries and Intellectual Property Protection

In the ever-evolving realm of economics, few phenomena have captured the attention of economists, politicians, diplomats, and scholars like the rise of high-tech industries and the importance of intellectual property protection. This subchapter delves into the fascinating journey of China's economic experiment and how it has successfully harnessed capitalism within a communist regime, with a specific focus on the growth and impact of high-tech industries and the crucial role played by intellectual property protection.

China's economic transformation has been nothing short of remarkable, and much of its success can be attributed to market-oriented reforms. The introduction of free-market principles and the encouragement of foreign direct investments have played a pivotal role in driving economic growth. These reforms have not only facilitated the inflow of capital but also allowed for the transfer of cutting-edge technologies and managerial expertise, enabling the rapid development of high-tech industries.

Special Economic Zones (SEZs) have been instrumental in China's economic success story. These zones have served as testing grounds for market-oriented reforms, offering favorable policies and incentives to both domestic and foreign businesses. Their establishment has not only attracted foreign investments but also fostered the growth of high-tech industries by providing a conducive environment for innovation, research, and development.

The integration of state-owned enterprises (SOEs) into a capitalist economic system has been a crucial aspect of China's economic experiment. By subjecting these enterprises to market forces and encouraging competition, China has effectively transformed them into dynamic and efficient entities. This integration has played a pivotal role in the development of high-tech industries, as these enterprises have been at the forefront of technological advancements and innovation.

China's transition from a planned to a market economy has presented both challenges and opportunities. The development of entrepreneurship and the flourishing private sector have been key drivers of economic growth. However, this transition has also brought about income inequality and social disparities, highlighting the need for inclusive growth policies and social safety nets.

Innovation and technological advancements have been central to China's economic achievements. The country has made significant strides in research and development, fostering an environment conducive to innovation and intellectual property protection. The rise of high-tech industries has catapulted China to the forefront of global technological advancements, challenging traditional economic powerhouses.

Globalization has also played a significant role in China's economic experiment. The country's integration into the global economy has allowed for the transfer of knowledge, technology, and capital, further fueling its economic growth. However, challenges such as protectionism and trade disputes have also emerged, necessitating the need for strategic policies to navigate these complexities.

The sustainability of China's economic model and its implications for future development remain a topic of intense debate. While the country has achieved remarkable economic growth, ensuring long-term sustainability and addressing environmental concerns will be critical.

In conclusion, the rise of high-tech industries and the protection of intellectual property rights have been integral to China's economic success story. Through market-oriented reforms, foreign investments, the establishment of SEZs, the integration of SOEs, and a focus on innovation, China has emerged as a global powerhouse in the high-tech sector. However, challenges such as income inequality, social disparities, and environmental sustainability must be addressed to ensure the long-term success of China's economic experiment.

Collaboration between Government, Academia, and Industry

In the remarkable journey of the China Economic Experiment, one crucial element that has contributed to its success is the collaboration between the government, academia, and industry. This unique partnership has played a pivotal role in driving China's economic growth, fostering innovation, and ensuring the sustainability of its economic model.

The Chinese government, recognizing the importance of knowledge and research in economic development, has actively promoted collaboration between academia and industry. By establishing research institutes, universities, and think tanks, the government has created a conducive environment for the exchange of ideas and the development of innovative solutions. Through funding and policy support, the government has encouraged researchers and scholars to work closely with industry players, driving technological advancements and facilitating the transfer of knowledge from academia to the market.

Industry, on the other hand, has been quick to embrace this collaboration, recognizing the value of research and development in gaining a competitive edge. By collaborating with academic institutions, businesses have gained access to cutting-edge research, expertise, and talent. This symbiotic relationship has enabled industry players to develop new products, improve efficiency, and enhance their global competitiveness.

The collaboration between government, academia, and industry has also been instrumental in the development of entrepreneurship and the private sector in China's economy. Through programs such as incubators, startup funds, and mentorship initiatives, the government has fostered a supportive ecosystem for entrepreneurs. Academic institutions have played a vital role in nurturing entrepreneurial talent, providing guidance and resources to aspiring business leaders. Industry, in turn, has acted as a catalyst, providing funding, expertise, and market access to startups, allowing them to thrive and contribute to China's economic growth.

Furthermore, this collaboration has been instrumental in addressing the challenges and opportunities of China's transition from a planned to a market economy. By bringing together the government's policy expertise, academia's research capabilities, and industry's market insights, stakeholders have been able to navigate the complex terrain of economic reforms effectively. This collaboration has allowed for the formulation of comprehensive policies, the identification of potential pitfalls, and the implementation of measures to mitigate risks.

Looking ahead, the collaboration between government, academia, and industry will continue to play a crucial role in shaping China's economic future. As China strives to maintain its growth trajectory, innovation and technological advancements will be paramount. By fostering collaboration, the government can ensure that research and development efforts are aligned with industry needs, driving innovation and propelling China's economic achievements.

In conclusion, the collaboration between government, academia, and industry has been a key driver of the China Economic Experiment's success. This partnership has facilitated the exchange of knowledge, driven innovation, and fostered the development of entrepreneurship and the private sector. As China faces new challenges and opportunities, collaboration will remain essential in ensuring the sustainability of its economic model and fostering future development.

China's Global Leadership in Emerging Technologies

China's economic experiment has not only transformed the country's domestic economy but also positioned it as a global leader in emerging technologies. This subchapter explores the factors that have contributed to China's rise in this field and the implications for the global economy.

Over the past few decades, China has heavily invested in research and development, creating an environment that fosters technological innovation. The government's focus on science and technology has resulted in significant advancements in areas such as artificial intelligence, 5G technology, biotechnology, and renewable energy. China is now at the forefront of these emerging technologies, challenging the traditional dominance of the West.

One of the key drivers of China's technological leadership is the role of foreign investments. The government has actively encouraged foreign companies to invest in China, providing them with incentives and access to the vast domestic market. This has not only brought in capital but also facilitated technology transfer, enabling Chinese companies to acquire cutting-edge technologies and expertise.

Special Economic Zones (SEZs) have played a crucial role in China's economic success and technological advancements. These zones, with their relaxed regulations and preferential policies, have attracted foreign investors and fostered innovation. SEZs have served as testing grounds for market-oriented reforms and have provided a fertile ground for the development of emerging technologies.

Furthermore, the integration of state-owned enterprises (SOEs) into a capitalist economic system has propelled China's technological advancements. By introducing market-oriented reforms in SOEs, the government has encouraged innovation and efficiency. This has allowed Chinese companies to compete globally and develop their technological capabilities.

The development of entrepreneurship and the private sector have also been instrumental in China's technological achievements. The government's support for startups and innovation-driven enterprises has created a vibrant ecosystem where new ideas can flourish. This has led to the emergence of numerous successful Chinese tech companies, such as Alibaba and Tencent, which are now global players in their respective fields.

China's transition from a planned to a market economy has presented both challenges and opportunities in the realm of technology. While the market-oriented approach has fueled innovation and technological advancements, it has also given rise to income inequality and social disparities. The government is now facing the challenge of balancing economic development with social stability, ensuring that the benefits of technological progress are shared by all.

China's technological achievements have been further amplified by globalization. The country has actively engaged with the global economy, attracting foreign talent, and collaborating with international partners. This has created a virtuous cycle where China's technological advancements drive economic growth, which, in turn, attracts more foreign investments and talent.

The sustainability of China's economic model and its implications for future development are important considerations. As China continues to lead in emerging technologies, it must also address environmental concerns and ensure long-term sustainable development. The government's commitment to green technologies and renewable energy sources is a step in the right direction, but more efforts are needed to mitigate the environmental impact of rapid technological advancements.

In conclusion, China's global leadership in emerging technologies is a testament to the success of its economic experiment. By embracing market-oriented reforms, attracting foreign investments, promoting entrepreneurship, and investing in research and development, China has positioned itself as a technological powerhouse. The implications of China's technological advancements are far-reaching, with potential impacts on the global economy, social dynamics, and the environment. As economists, politicians, diplomats, and scholars, it is crucial to closely monitor China's trajectory and understand the opportunities and challenges it presents for the future.

# Chapter 9: The Impact of Globalization on China's Economic Experiment

China's Integration into the Global Economy

China's integration into the global economy has been a remarkable phenomenon that has captivated economists, politicians, diplomats, and scholars alike. The country's economic experiment, utilizing a capitalist economic system within a communist regime, has yielded tremendous success, sparking interest in various aspects of this unique model.

One of the key factors contributing to China's economic growth has been the impact of market-oriented reforms. By gradually embracing market principles and allowing private enterprise to flourish, China has experienced unprecedented economic expansion. These reforms have encouraged innovation, efficiency, and competition, propelling the country to become the world's second-largest economy.

Foreign investments have played a crucial role in China's economic transformation. The inflow of foreign capital has not only provided China with additional resources for development but has also facilitated knowledge and technology transfer. The establishment of Special Economic Zones (SEZs) has been instrumental in attracting foreign direct investment and fostering export-oriented industries, leading to China's increased global competitiveness.

Another significant aspect of China's economic success has been the integration of state-owned enterprises (SOEs) into a capitalist economic system. Through reforms aimed at improving efficiency and profitability, these once inefficient and bureaucratic entities have been transformed into dynamic and competitive market players, contributing to the overall growth of the Chinese economy.

The development of entrepreneurship and the private sector have also been crucial in China's economic transformation. The government's recognition of the importance of entrepreneurship and its support for private enterprises have created a vibrant business environment. This has not only stimulated innovation but also provided employment opportunities, contributing to poverty reduction and social stability.

However, China's transition from a planned to a market economy has not been without challenges. The country has had to navigate issues such as income inequality and social disparities, which have emerged as unintended consequences of rapid economic growth. The government has made efforts to address these issues through various social policies, but further steps are required to ensure a more equitable distribution of wealth and opportunities.

Innovation and technological advancements have played a pivotal role in China's economic achievements. The country's commitment to research and development, coupled with its large pool of skilled labor, has led to breakthroughs in various sectors, enhancing productivity and competitiveness. China's emergence as a global leader in technology and innovation has further solidified its position in the global economy.

Globalization has undoubtedly influenced China's economic experiment. The country's integration into the global economy has opened up new markets, facilitated trade, and enhanced economic cooperation with other nations. However, it has also exposed China to external shocks, necessitating the need for robust policy responses to maintain stability and sustain growth.

The sustainability of China's economic model and its implications for future development are topics of great significance. As the country continues to evolve, it must address environmental challenges, promote sustainable development, and ensure the well-being of its citizens.

Striking a delicate balance between economic growth and social and environmental considerations will be critical for China's long-term success.

In conclusion, China's integration into the global economy has been a success story of capitalism in a communist regime. The country's market-oriented reforms, foreign investments, Special Economic Zones, and the integration of state-owned enterprises have propelled its economic growth. The development of entrepreneurship, innovation, and technological advancements have further contributed to its achievements. However, challenges such as income inequality, social disparities, and environmental sustainability must be addressed to ensure a prosperous and sustainable future for China.

The Belt and Road Initiative: China's Geopolitical and Economic Strategy

The Belt and Road Initiative (BRI) has emerged as a cornerstone of China's geopolitical and economic strategy in recent years. This ambitious initiative, proposed by Chinese President Xi Jinping in 2013, aims to connect Asia, Europe, and Africa through a network of infrastructure projects, trade routes, and economic cooperation. It has since become a focal point of China's foreign policy, shaping its relationships with neighboring countries and exerting a significant influence on global trade patterns.

From an economic standpoint, the BRI holds immense potential for both China and the countries involved. By promoting connectivity and infrastructure development, it seeks to enhance trade and investment flows, foster economic growth, and create new market opportunities. Economists and scholars have hailed the BRI as a catalyst for regional integration and a means to boost global economic development.

The BRI also aligns with the core principles of China's economic experiment. Over the years, China has successfully utilized a capitalist economic system within a communist regime, resulting in unprecedented economic growth. The market-oriented reforms implemented in the late 1970s played a crucial role in driving this growth, unleashing the entrepreneurial spirit and private sector development. The BRI builds upon these successes by encouraging further market-oriented reforms and promoting entrepreneurship in the countries involved.

Foreign investments have been instrumental in China's economic transformation, and the BRI aims to attract even more investment by creating a conducive environment for businesses. Special Economic Zones (SEZs) have played a pivotal role in China's economic success, and the BRI seeks to replicate their success by establishing similar zones along the Belt and Road. These zones offer numerous incentives, including tax breaks, streamlined regulations, and access to infrastructure, to attract foreign investors and stimulate economic activity.

The integration of state-owned enterprises (SOEs) into a capitalist economic system has been another key aspect of China's economic experiment. The BRI provides an avenue for these SOEs to expand their operations overseas, contributing to their transformation and fostering international cooperation.

Innovation and technological advancements have been vital drivers of China's economic achievements, and the BRI aims to promote collaboration in these areas. By facilitating the exchange of ideas, knowledge, and technology, it seeks to accelerate innovation and create a more competitive and sustainable economic model.

However, the BRI is not without its challenges. The scale and complexity of the initiative present significant logistical and financial obstacles. Additionally, concerns have been raised regarding debt sustainability, environmental impacts, and the potential for geopolitical tensions. Policymakers, economists, and scholars must carefully navigate these challenges to ensure the long-term success and sustainability of the BRI.

In conclusion, the Belt and Road Initiative represents a pivotal component of China's geopolitical and economic strategy. It builds upon the successes of the China Economic Experiment, leveraging market-oriented reforms, foreign investments, special economic zones, state-owned enterprise integration, entrepreneurship, innovation, and globalization. While the initiative offers immense opportunities for regional integration and economic development, it also poses challenges that must be addressed to ensure its long-term success. Policymakers, economists, politicians, diplomats, and scholars must closely examine the implications of the BRI for China's economic model and its potential impact on future development.

Trade Wars and Protectionism: Challenges and Responses

In recent years, the world has witnessed an escalating trend of trade wars and protectionism, with major economies engaging in tit-for-tat tariff hikes and other restrictive trade measures. These developments have posed significant challenges to the global economy and have particularly important implications for China, given its unique economic experiment of using a capitalist economic system within a communist regime. This subchapter explores the challenges and responses that China has faced in the context of trade wars and protectionism.

As economists, politicians, diplomats, and scholars, it is crucial to understand the successes of the China Economic Experiment and how it has enabled the country to achieve remarkable economic growth. Market-oriented reforms have played a crucial role in this success story, allowing China to transition from a planned to a market economy. These reforms have attracted foreign investments, which have been instrumental in driving China's economic transformation. The establishment of Special Economic Zones (SEZs) has further enhanced China's economic success, providing a testing ground for innovative policies and attracting foreign investments.

However, the integration of state-owned enterprises (SOEs) into a capitalist economic system has presented unique challenges. The dominance of SOEs in strategic sectors has raised concerns about fair competition and market distortions. China has been actively addressing these challenges through various reforms, including improving corporate governance and promoting market-oriented practices within SOEs.

The development of entrepreneurship and the private sector in China's economy has been another important aspect of its economic achievements. Chinese entrepreneurs have demonstrated remarkable resilience and innovation, contributing significantly to economic growth. However, the transition from a planned to a market economy has also presented challenges and opportunities. China has been working to create a favorable environment for entrepreneurship, including strengthening intellectual property rights and reducing bureaucratic hurdles.

In the face of trade wars and protectionism, China has responded with a range of strategies. It has sought to diversify its trade partners and expand its market access through initiatives like the Belt and Road Initiative. China has also emphasized the role of innovation and technological advancements in driving its economic achievements, investing heavily in research and development and promoting high-tech industries.

Globalization has played a crucial role in China's economic experiment, enabling it to integrate into the global value chains and become the world's largest trading nation. However, the impact of globalization on China's economy has also led to income inequality and social disparities. China has recognized these challenges and has implemented measures to address them, including poverty alleviation programs and social welfare reforms.

Looking ahead, the sustainability of China's economic model and its implications for future development is a key concern. As China continues to navigate the challenges of trade wars and protectionism, it must ensure that its economic model remains adaptable and resilient. This will require ongoing reforms, including addressing issues of income inequality, promoting sustainable development, and fostering innovation.

In conclusion, the challenges posed by trade wars and protectionism have tested China's economic experiment. However, China has responded with determination and resilience, leveraging its unique economic model to navigate these challenges. As economists, politicians, diplomats, and scholars, it is crucial to closely monitor these developments and learn from the successes and failures of the China Economic Experiment, as they will undoubtedly shape the future of global economics and governance.

The Future of Globalization and China's Position

In recent decades, China has emerged as a global economic powerhouse, defying traditional expectations and reshaping the global economic landscape. As the world's second-largest economy and a major player in international trade, China's position in the future of globalization is of paramount importance. This subchapter will explore the implications of China's economic experiment on globalization and its role in shaping the future.

China's economic success is a testament to the effectiveness of using a capitalist economic system within a communist regime. By embracing market-oriented reforms, China has achieved remarkable economic growth over the years, becoming a model for other developing nations. These reforms have unleashed the potential of the Chinese economy, leading to increased productivity, efficiency, and competitiveness.

Foreign investments have played a crucial role in China's economic transformation. By attracting foreign capital and expertise, China has been able to modernize its industries, upgrade its infrastructure, and develop new technologies. The establishment of Special Economic Zones (SEZs) has been instrumental in attracting foreign investments, providing a conducive environment for businesses to thrive and contributing to China's economic success.

The integration of state-owned enterprises (SOEs) into a capitalist economic system has been a significant milestone in China's economic experiment. Through reforms, these enterprises have become more market-oriented, improving efficiency and profitability. The government's efforts to promote entrepreneurship and foster the growth of the private sector have also been key drivers of China's economic achievements.

However, China's transition from a planned to a market economy has not been without challenges. The country has had to grapple with issues such as income inequality and social disparities, resulting from the coexistence of a capitalist-communist hybrid system. Addressing these challenges is crucial for ensuring the sustainability of China's economic model and fostering inclusive growth.

Innovation and technological advancements have been pivotal in China's economic achievements. The country has made significant strides in industries such as artificial intelligence, e-commerce, and renewable energy, positioning itself as a global leader in innovation.

Leveraging these advancements will be critical in maintaining China's competitive edge and driving future economic development.

Globalization has played a significant role in China's economic experiment. By expanding its global reach through trade and investment, China has become deeply integrated into the global economy. However, the future of globalization faces uncertainties, with rising protectionism and geopolitical tensions. China's position in this evolving global order will be crucial, as it seeks to balance its domestic priorities with its commitment to open markets and international cooperation.

In conclusion, China's economic experiment has defied expectations and positioned the country as a global economic powerhouse. The successes achieved through the use of a capitalist economic system within a communist regime, market-oriented reforms, foreign investments, and innovation have propelled China's economic growth. However, challenges such as income inequality and social disparities must be addressed to ensure the sustainability of China's economic model. As globalization faces uncertainties, China's role in shaping the future of globalization will be instrumental, as it strives to maintain its competitive edge while navigating an evolving global order.

# Chapter 10: Income Inequality and Social Disparities in China's Capitalist-Communist Hybrid System

The Gini Coefficient and Wealth Distribution

In the pursuit of understanding China's economic experiment, one cannot overlook the crucial role of the Gini coefficient in analyzing wealth distribution. This subchapter delves into the significance of the Gini coefficient in China's capitalist-communist hybrid system and its implications for the country's future development.

The Gini coefficient is a widely accepted measure of income inequality, ranging from 0 to 1, with 0 representing perfect equality and 1 representing extreme inequality. By examining this coefficient, economists, politicians, diplomats, and scholars can gain insights into China's progress in bridging the gap between the rich and the poor.

China's economic reforms have undoubtedly led to remarkable economic growth, lifting millions out of poverty. However, this growth has also resulted in increasing income disparities. The Gini coefficient in China has risen significantly over the years, indicating a widening wealth gap. This phenomenon has raised concerns among policymakers, economists, and social scientists about the long-term sustainability of China's economic model.

Addressing income inequality is imperative to maintain social stability and ensure sustainable economic development. China's leaders are aware of this challenge and have implemented various policies to tackle wealth disparities. These initiatives include redistributive taxation, social welfare programs, and targeted poverty alleviation projects. The effectiveness of these policies in reducing inequality can be measured by monitoring changes in the Gini coefficient over time.

Moreover, understanding the factors driving income inequality is crucial for devising effective policies. The impact of market-oriented reforms, the role of foreign investments, the influence of Special Economic Zones (SEZs), and the integration of state-owned enterprises (SOEs) into a capitalist economic system all play a role in shaping wealth distribution. By analyzing these factors in conjunction with the Gini coefficient, policymakers can identify areas that require further attention and implement targeted measures.

The sustainability of China's economic model hinges on addressing income inequality. Failure to do so could undermine social cohesion, hinder further economic development, and jeopardize China's future growth prospects. As economists, politicians, diplomats, and scholars delve into the intricacies of the Gini coefficient and wealth distribution, they contribute to the ongoing dialogue surrounding China's economic experiment. By shedding light on the challenges and opportunities presented by income inequality, they pave the way for a more inclusive and sustainable future for China's economy.

Urban-Rural Divide: Bridging the Gap

As China continues to undergo its remarkable economic transformation, one pressing issue that needs to be addressed is the urban-rural divide. This subchapter delves into the challenges and opportunities associated with bridging this gap in order to achieve a more equitable and inclusive growth.

The urban-rural divide in China is a complex issue that stems from historical, social, and economic factors. With rapid urbanization and the concentration of economic opportunities in urban areas, rural regions have been left behind, leading to stark disparities in income, access to basic services, and quality of life. This divide not only hinders social cohesion but also poses a threat to China's long-term sustainable development.

To bridge this gap, it is crucial to understand the underlying causes and implement comprehensive policies that address the unique challenges faced by rural communities. One approach is to focus on the development of rural industries and agriculture, encouraging innovation and technological advancements in these sectors. By promoting entrepreneurship and supporting the growth of the private sector in rural areas, the government can create job opportunities and improve living standards for rural residents.

Additionally, the integration of state-owned enterprises (SOEs) into a capitalist economic system can play a pivotal role in narrowing the urban-rural divide. By encouraging SOEs to invest in rural areas and provide employment opportunities, the government can stimulate economic growth and reduce regional disparities.

Furthermore, the development of Special Economic Zones (SEZs) in rural regions can attract foreign investments and facilitate the transfer of technology and knowledge. These zones can serve as catalysts for economic growth, creating employment opportunities and improving infrastructure in rural areas.

However, bridging the urban-rural divide requires not only economic measures but also social policies that promote income redistribution, access to education, healthcare, and social protection. The government should prioritize the provision of basic services in rural areas and invest in infrastructure development to connect rural communities with urban centers.

Moreover, the sustainability of China's economic model depends on addressing income inequality and social disparities. By ensuring that the benefits of economic growth are shared more equitably, China can foster social stability and secure its long-term economic development.

In conclusion, bridging the urban-rural divide in China is a complex task that requires multi-faceted strategies and comprehensive policies. By promoting rural industries, integrating SOEs, developing SEZs, and implementing social policies that prioritize inclusivity and equal access to opportunities, China can achieve a more balanced and sustainable economic growth, ensuring a brighter future for all its citizens.

Social Safety Nets and Poverty Alleviation Programs

In the pursuit of economic growth and development, China has recognized the importance of addressing social disparities and reducing poverty. The implementation of social safety nets and poverty alleviation programs has played a crucial role in ensuring a more inclusive and equitable society within China's capitalist-communist hybrid system.

One of the key successes of the China Economic Experiment has been the establishment of robust social safety nets. These safety nets have provided a safety cushion for vulnerable populations, including the elderly, disabled, and unemployed. Through the provision of social assistance programs, such as the Minimum Livelihood Guarantee, China has been able to reduce extreme poverty rates and improve the living conditions of millions of individuals.

Furthermore, poverty alleviation programs have been instrumental in lifting millions out of poverty and narrowing the income gap. The Chinese government has implemented targeted poverty alleviation initiatives, focusing on areas with high poverty rates and vulnerable populations. These programs have included infrastructure development, access to education and healthcare, and vocational training, aiming to improve the overall well-being and economic prospects of those living in poverty.

Foreign investments have also played a significant role in supporting China's poverty alleviation efforts. The inflow of foreign capital has facilitated the development of industries and job creation, which in turn has contributed to poverty reduction. Additionally, foreign investments have enabled the transfer of knowledge, technology, and skills, fostering innovation and productivity growth, ultimately leading to improved living standards for the Chinese population.

The integration of state-owned enterprises (SOEs) into a capitalist economic system has also contributed to poverty alleviation. By subjecting SOEs to market forces and competition, China has incentivized efficiency and innovation, which have led to increased productivity and job opportunities. This has been particularly beneficial for individuals in rural areas who have sought employment opportunities outside of agriculture.

However, despite these achievements, challenges remain. Income inequality continues to be a pressing issue within China's economic model. While poverty rates have decreased significantly, the gap between the rich and the poor has widened. It is crucial for policymakers to address this issue through progressive taxation, redistribution measures, and targeted social programs to ensure equitable growth and a more inclusive society.

In conclusion, the implementation of social safety nets and poverty alleviation programs has been integral to China's economic success. By addressing social disparities and reducing poverty, China has created a more inclusive and equitable society. However, it is important to continue addressing income inequality and sustain the success of these programs to ensure a prosperous and sustainable future for China's economic model.

Addressing Social Disparities and Promoting Inclusive Growth

In the journey towards becoming the world's second-largest economy, China has undoubtedly achieved remarkable economic success through its unique capitalist-communist hybrid system. However, this success has also brought to light various challenges, including income inequality and social disparities. To ensure sustainable development, it is crucial to address these issues and promote inclusive growth in the Chinese economy.

The China Economic Experiment has demonstrated the power of using a capitalist economic system within a communist regime. Market-oriented reforms have played a significant role in driving China's remarkable economic growth. These reforms have enabled the country to embrace globalization, attract foreign investments, and create Special Economic Zones (SEZs) that have acted as catalysts for economic success.

However, it is essential to recognize that this transformation has not been without its consequences. Income inequality has emerged as a significant concern in China's capitalist-communist hybrid system. This has led to social disparities, with certain regions and segments of the population benefiting more than others. It is imperative for economists, politicians, diplomats, and scholars to address these disparities and ensure that the benefits of economic growth are shared more equitably.

One way to tackle social disparities is through the integration of state-owned enterprises (SOEs) into the capitalist economic system. By introducing market-oriented reforms in these enterprises, China can promote efficiency, competition, and innovation, thus creating a level playing field for all participants in the economy.

Furthermore, the development of entrepreneurship and the private sector can also contribute to addressing social disparities. Encouraging the growth of small and medium-sized enterprises (SMEs) and supporting entrepreneurial activities can create more opportunities for individuals and communities to participate in and benefit from economic growth.

Additionally, innovation and technological advancements play a crucial role in promoting inclusive growth. By investing in research and development, China can foster innovation-driven economic growth, creating new industries and job opportunities that can benefit a broader range of individuals.

As China continues its transition from a planned to a market economy, it is vital to recognize the challenges and opportunities that lie ahead. Balancing economic growth with social development, environmental sustainability, and social equity requires careful policymaking and collaboration among various stakeholders.

The sustainability of China's economic model will have significant implications for future development. As the country navigates the complexities of globalization and adapts to changing global dynamics, it must continuously evaluate and adjust its economic policies to ensure that they align with the goals of inclusive growth and social harmony.

In conclusion, addressing social disparities and promoting inclusive growth is a critical aspect of the China Economic Experiment. By recognizing and tackling income inequality and social disparities, China can ensure sustainable and balanced development, benefiting all segments of society. This requires a comprehensive approach that integrates market-oriented reforms, supports entrepreneurship and innovation, and fosters collaboration among various stakeholders. Only by addressing these challenges can China continue to build on its economic success and shape a prosperous future for its people.

# Chapter 11: The Sustainability of China's Economic Model and its Implications for Future Development

Environmental Challenges and Green Growth

China's remarkable economic transformation has come at a cost to its environment. As the country's rapid industrialization and urbanization have propelled it to become the world's second-largest economy, it has also faced significant environmental challenges. However, China has recognized the importance of addressing these challenges and embracing green growth as a means to ensure the sustainability of its economic model.

One of the key environmental challenges China faces is air pollution. The country's heavy reliance on coal for energy generation has resulted in severe air pollution in many of its cities. The government has implemented various measures to tackle this issue, including the introduction of stricter emission standards, promoting renewable energy sources, and implementing pollution control measures.

Water scarcity is another pressing concern for China. Rapid economic growth and urbanization have strained the country's water resources, leading to water pollution and depletion. To address this challenge, China has implemented policies to improve water efficiency, increase investments in water conservation projects, and strengthen water management practices.

China's rapid urbanization has also resulted in the loss of natural habitats and biodiversity. The conversion of agricultural land into urban areas and industrial sites has led to habitat fragmentation and the decline of many species. The Chinese government has recognized the importance of biodiversity conservation and has established protected areas and implemented measures to promote ecological restoration and sustainable land use.

Recognizing the need for green growth, China has made significant investments in renewable energy. The country has become the world's largest producer of solar panels and wind turbines, and it has also invested heavily in hydropower and nuclear energy. These efforts have not only helped to reduce fossil fuel dependence but have also positioned China as a global leader in renewable energy technology.

Furthermore, China has been actively promoting green technologies and industries through policies and incentives. The government has provided support for the development of electric vehicles, sustainable agriculture, and clean technologies. This has not only helped to reduce environmental impact but has also created new opportunities for economic growth and job creation.

In conclusion, while China's economic experiment has brought immense success in terms of economic growth and poverty reduction, it has also presented significant environmental challenges. However, China has recognized the importance of addressing these challenges and is actively pursuing green growth as a means to ensure the sustainability of its economic model. Through various policies and investments in renewable energy, environmental conservation, and green technologies, China is positioning itself as a global leader in sustainable development. The success of China's transition to a green economy will not only benefit its own people but also serve as an inspiration and example for other countries facing similar challenges.

Energy Transition and Renewable Energy Investments

The China Economic Experiment: A Success Story of Capitalism in a Communist Regime

Introduction:

As the world faces the challenges of climate change and the need for sustainable development, the transition to renewable energy sources has become a global priority. In the context of China's economic transformation, this subchapter explores the country's energy transition and its investments in renewable energy. It highlights the successes, challenges, and implications of this transition for China's economic model and its future development.

Renewable Energy Investments:

China's economic experiment has witnessed a remarkable shift towards renewable energy investments. The country has become a global leader in clean energy production, surpassing all other nations in renewable energy capacity. This transition has been driven by significant investments in solar, wind, hydro, and nuclear power. China's commitment to renewable energy is reflected in its ambitious targets and policies, such as the 2060 carbon neutrality pledge.

Successes:

China's investments in renewable energy have yielded several successes. Firstly, the country has reduced its reliance on fossil fuels, enhancing its energy security and reducing pollution levels. Secondly, it has created a thriving renewable energy industry, generating employment opportunities and attracting foreign investments. China's dominance in the manufacturing of solar panels and wind turbines exemplifies its success in this sector.

Challenges:

Despite its successes, China's energy transition faces challenges. One major challenge is the integration of renewable energy into the existing grid infrastructure. The intermittent nature of renewable energy sources requires the development of advanced storage technologies and a smarter grid system. Additionally, the transition may create social disruptions in regions heavily reliant on fossil fuel industries, necessitating careful planning and support for affected communities.

Implications for China's Economic Model:

The energy transition and renewable energy investments have profound implications for China's economic model. Firstly, it demonstrates the ability of a communist regime to embrace market-oriented reforms and adapt to global trends. China's pursuit of renewable energy aligns with its broader economic goals of sustainable development and global leadership. Secondly, it highlights the potential for innovation and technological advancements in driving economic growth and transformation.

Future Development:

The sustainability of China's economic model hinges on the successful energy transition and renewable energy investments. By reducing its carbon footprint and promoting clean technologies, China can position itself as a global leader in the fight against climate change. The country's commitment to sustainable development will attract further foreign investments and contribute to its long-term economic growth.

Conclusion:

China's energy transition and investments in renewable energy exemplify the successes and challenges of its economic experiment. By embracing market-oriented reforms and adapting to global trends, China has demonstrated the viability of a capitalist economic system within a communist regime. The country's commitment to renewable energy not only enhances its energy security and reduces pollution but also creates new economic opportunities and positions China as a global leader in sustainable development. The successful transition to renewable energy is crucial for the sustainability of China's economic model and its implications for future development.

Balancing Economic Growth with Social Welfare

In the realm of economic development, the Chinese experience has emerged as a remarkable success story, showcasing the efficacy of a capitalist economic system within a communist regime. China's journey towards economic prosperity has been shaped by various factors, including market-oriented reforms, foreign investments, Special Economic Zones (SEZs), the integration of state-owned enterprises (SOEs), the development of entrepreneurship and the private sector, as well as innovation and technological advancements. However, as China continues its transition from a planned to a market economy, it faces the challenge of balancing economic growth with social welfare.

The impact of market-oriented reforms on China's economic growth cannot be overstated. By liberalizing markets, reducing government intervention, and promoting healthy competition, China has witnessed an unprecedented surge in its gross domestic product (GDP) over the past few decades. These reforms have not only fostered economic growth but have also brought millions of people out of poverty, leading to a significant improvement in living standards.

Foreign investments have played a crucial role in China's economic transformation. Through the establishment of joint ventures and the infusion of capital and technology, foreign companies have contributed to the modernization of China's industries. Additionally, the presence of foreign firms has created employment opportunities, enhanced productivity, and facilitated the transfer of knowledge and skills.

Special Economic Zones (SEZs) have acted as catalysts for China's economic success. By offering preferential policies and incentives to domestic and foreign investors, SEZs have attracted substantial investments, stimulated exports, and propelled economic growth in specific regions. The success of SEZs has prompted the replication of their model across the country, leading to regional development and improved living standards.

The integration of state-owned enterprises (SOEs) into a capitalist economic system has been a significant milestone in China's economic transformation. By subjecting SOEs to market forces and introducing competition, the efficiency and performance of these enterprises have improved. The partial privatization of SOEs has also increased their accountability and incentivized innovation.

The development of entrepreneurship and the private sector has been instrumental in driving China's economic growth. The rise of small and medium-sized enterprises (SMEs) has created employment opportunities, fostered innovation, and contributed to the diversification of the economy. The entrepreneurial spirit and the dynamism of the private sector have been crucial in propelling China's economic success.

However, China's transition to a market economy has not been without challenges. Income inequality and social disparities have emerged as pressing issues. The rapid economic growth has widened the gap between the rich and the poor, leading to social unrest and discontent. Addressing income inequality and ensuring social welfare are critical for sustainable and inclusive growth.

Furthermore, the sustainability of China's economic model and its implications for future development are subjects of great importance. As China further integrates into the global economy, it must navigate the challenges posed by globalization, including increased competition and environmental concerns. Balancing economic growth with social welfare will be crucial in ensuring long-term sustainability and equitable development.

In conclusion, the Chinese economic experiment has been a triumph of capitalism within a communist regime. Through market-oriented reforms, foreign investments, the establishment of SEZs, the integration of SOEs, the development of entrepreneurship and the private sector, as well as innovation and technological advancements, China has achieved remarkable economic growth. However, the challenge lies in striking a balance between economic growth and social welfare, addressing income inequality, and ensuring the sustainability of its economic model for future development.

Lessons from China's Economic Experiment for other Developing Countries

China's economic experiment of combining a capitalist economic system within a communist regime has garnered significant attention from economists, politicians, diplomats, and scholars worldwide. The successes achieved and challenges faced by China provide valuable lessons for other developing countries seeking to transform their economies. This subchapter aims to explore these lessons and their implications.

One of the key lessons from China's economic experiment is the importance of market-oriented reforms in driving economic growth. By gradually introducing market mechanisms and liberalizing the economy, China witnessed remarkable growth rates and lifted millions out of poverty. This lesson emphasizes the need for other developing countries to prioritize market-oriented reforms to unleash their economic potential.

Foreign investments played a crucial role in China's economic transformation. Opening up to foreign capital and technology transfer allowed China to attract significant investments, which fueled its economic growth. Other developing countries can learn from China's experience and actively seek foreign investments to boost their own economies.

Special Economic Zones (SEZs) played a pivotal role in China's economic success. These zones, which offered preferential policies and incentives to attract foreign investments, served as testing grounds for market-oriented reforms. Other developing countries can establish similar zones to attract investments and facilitate economic transformation.

The integration of state-owned enterprises (SOEs) into a capitalist economic system was a significant challenge for China. Lessons can be drawn from China's experience in reforming and modernizing SOEs, ensuring their efficiency and competitiveness within a market-oriented economy.

China's economic experiment also witnessed the development of entrepreneurship and a vibrant private sector. Encouraging the growth of entrepreneurship and supporting the private sector are crucial for other developing countries to achieve sustainable economic development.

The transition from a planned to a market economy posed both challenges and opportunities for China. Understanding the hurdles faced by China during this transition can help other developing countries navigate their own economic transformations effectively.

Innovation and technological advancements played a vital role in China's economic achievements. Other developing countries should prioritize investments in research and development and foster innovation to drive economic growth.

The impact of globalization on China's economic experiment cannot be ignored. China's integration into global markets and its active participation in international trade have been instrumental in its economic success. Developing countries should embrace globalization and actively engage in international trade to maximize their economic potential.

China's capitalist-communist hybrid system has resulted in income inequality and social disparities. It is essential for other developing countries to address these challenges and pursue inclusive growth to ensure social stability and harmony.

Finally, the sustainability of China's economic model and its implications for future development should be carefully analyzed. Other developing countries can learn from China's experience in ensuring the long-term viability of their economic models.

In conclusion, the lessons from China's economic experiment offer valuable insights for other developing countries. By focusing on market-oriented reforms, attracting foreign investments, establishing special economic zones, reforming state-owned enterprises, nurturing entrepreneurship, embracing innovation, engaging in globalization, addressing income inequality, and ensuring sustainability, developing countries can draw inspiration from China's success story and pave their own path to economic prosperity.

Conclusion: Reflections on China's Economic Experiment and its Global Significance

Assessing the Successes and Failures of the China Economic Experiment

China's economic experiment of blending capitalism into a communist regime has been a subject of great interest and debate among economists, politicians, diplomats, and scholars. In this subchapter, we will delve into the various aspects of this experiment to assess its successes and failures, providing a comprehensive understanding of the path China has taken.

One of the most remarkable successes of the China Economic Experiment has been the utilization of a capitalist economic system within a communist dictatorship. By adopting market-oriented reforms, China has experienced unprecedented economic growth over the past few decades. These reforms have allowed for increased efficiency, productivity, and innovation, propelling China to become the world's second-largest economy.

Foreign investments have played a crucial role in China's economic transformation. The opening up of China's markets and the establishment of Special Economic Zones (SEZs) have attracted significant foreign capital, technology, and expertise. This has not only fueled economic growth but also facilitated knowledge transfer, industrial upgrading, and the development of export-oriented industries.

The integration of state-owned enterprises (SOEs) into a capitalist economic system has been a complex process with both successes and failures. While some SOEs have successfully transitioned into competitive entities, others continue to face challenges in adapting to market forces. However, the overall reform efforts have improved efficiency, increased profitability, and created a more dynamic business environment.

China's economic experiment has also witnessed the emergence of entrepreneurship and the flourishing of the private sector. The government's support for small and medium-sized enterprises (SMEs) has encouraged innovation, job creation, and economic diversification. This has contributed to a more vibrant and dynamic economy.

However, transitioning from a planned to a market economy has not been without its challenges. China has faced issues such as corruption, income inequality, and social disparities. The government has been working towards addressing these challenges through various policy measures, including poverty alleviation programs and social welfare reforms.

Innovation and technological advancements have played a pivotal role in China's economic achievements. The country has invested heavily in research and development, resulting in breakthroughs in various sectors, including technology, manufacturing, and renewable energy. These advancements have enhanced China's global competitiveness and positioned it as a leader in innovation.

Globalization has also had a profound impact on China's economic experiment. The country has embraced international trade, becoming a major player in global supply chains. China's integration into the world economy has not only boosted its economic growth but also exposed it to various risks and challenges, such as fluctuations in global demand and trade tensions.

The sustainability of China's economic model remains a critical concern. Balancing economic growth with environmental protection, addressing income inequality, and ensuring social stability are ongoing priorities for the Chinese government. The implications of China's economic model for future development will depend on its ability to navigate these challenges effectively.

In conclusion, the China Economic Experiment has witnessed significant successes in utilizing a capitalist economic system within a communist regime. Market-oriented reforms, foreign investments, Special Economic Zones, the integration of state-owned enterprises, the development of entrepreneurship, and technological advancements have propelled China's economic growth. However, challenges such as income inequality, social disparities, and environmental sustainability remain. Assessing the successes and failures of this experiment is crucial for economists, politicians, diplomats, and scholars to understand the implications of China's economic model and its potential for future development.

Implications for Economic and Political Systems Worldwide

The China Economic Experiment: A Success Story of Capitalism in a Communist Regime

The rise of China as an economic powerhouse has captivated economists, politicians, diplomats, and scholars around the world. The unique blend of a capitalist economic system within a communist regime has defied conventional wisdom and challenged existing notions of economic and political systems. This subchapter delves into the implications of the China Economic Experiment on both economic and political systems worldwide.

One of the key takeaways from China's economic success is the potential of utilizing a capitalist economic system within a communist dictatorship. The successes of the China Economic Experiment highlight the adaptability and resilience of capitalism, even in a regime that traditionally opposes it. This challenges preconceived notions that capitalism can only thrive in a democratic environment, opening up new possibilities for economic development in countries with different political systems.

Market-oriented reforms have played a pivotal role in China's economic growth. By embracing market principles such as competition and private ownership, China has been able to unlock its economic potential and achieve rapid growth. This serves as a powerful example for other countries looking to jumpstart their economies and foster sustained development.

Foreign investments have played a crucial role in China's economic transformation. Opening up to foreign capital and expertise has allowed China to tap into global markets, attract multinational corporations, and benefit from technology transfers. The Chinese government's ability to strike a delicate balance between protecting national interests and welcoming foreign investments offers valuable insights for policymakers worldwide.

The establishment of Special Economic Zones (SEZs) in China has been instrumental in its economic success. These zones, with their unique regulatory frameworks and favorable investment conditions, have attracted both domestic and foreign businesses, promoting economic growth and innovation. The replication of this model in other countries could potentially spur economic development and attract foreign investments.

The integration of state-owned enterprises (SOEs) into a capitalist economic system has been a significant challenge for China. However, the successful transformation of some SOEs into efficient and competitive entities provides valuable lessons for other countries grappling with the issue of state-owned industries.

Furthermore, the development of entrepreneurship and the private sector has been vital in driving China's economic growth. The Chinese government's recognition of the importance of private enterprise and its efforts to create a conducive environment for entrepreneurship have led to a vibrant private sector that has become a driving force behind the country's economic success.

While China's transition from a planned to a market economy has presented numerous challenges, it has also opened up new opportunities. The ability to navigate these challenges and seize the opportunities associated with this transition will be crucial for countries looking to emulate China's success.

Innovation and technological advancements have played a pivotal role in China's economic achievements. By investing heavily in research and development and fostering a culture of innovation, China has become a global leader in areas such as artificial intelligence, renewable energy, and telecommunications.

Globalization has had a profound impact on China's economic experiment. The country's integration into the global economy has allowed it to become a major player in international trade and investment. China's experience offers valuable insights into the benefits and challenges of globalization for other countries.

However, China's capitalist-communist hybrid system has also given rise to income inequality and social disparities. Addressing these issues will be crucial to ensure the sustainability and inclusivity of China's economic model.

The sustainability of China's economic model and its implications for future development is a topic of great interest. As China continues to grow, questions arise about the long-term viability of its economic model and its ability to address pressing global challenges such as environmental sustainability and social welfare.

In conclusion, the China Economic Experiment has far-reaching implications for economic and political systems worldwide. It challenges traditional notions of economic development and political systems, offering valuable lessons for economists, politicians, diplomats, and scholars. The successes, challenges, and opportunities associated with the China Economic Experiment provide a rich tapestry of insights for those interested in understanding the potential of capitalism within a communist regime and the future of global economics and politics.

Lessons Learned and Recommendations for Future Development

In the dynamic and complex landscape of China's economic experiment, there are valuable lessons to be learned from its successes and challenges. This subchapter aims to provide insights and recommendations for future development, targeting economists, politicians, diplomats, and scholars interested in the intersections of capitalism and communism. It also caters to specific niches, such as the impacts of market-oriented reforms, foreign investments, Special Economic Zones (SEZs), state-owned enterprises (SOEs), entrepreneurship, innovation, globalization, income inequality, and the sustainability of China's economic model.

One crucial lesson from China's economic experiment is the successful utilization of a capitalist economic system within a communist dictatorship. The integration of market-oriented reforms has played a significant role in China's remarkable economic growth. Policymakers and economists should consider adopting similar reforms in other countries with similar contexts, ensuring careful planning and gradual implementation.

Foreign investments have been instrumental in China's economic transformation. Policymakers and diplomats should prioritize creating an environment conducive to foreign investment, including legal frameworks, intellectual property protection, and reducing bureaucratic hurdles. Encouraging technology transfers and collaborations between foreign and domestic entities can further enhance China's economic development.

Special Economic Zones (SEZs) have been pivotal in driving China's economic success. Policymakers should replicate the SEZ model in other regions, offering tax incentives, streamlined regulations, and infrastructure development to attract both domestic and foreign investments. Close monitoring and evaluation of SEZ activities can identify best practices to be replicated nationwide.

The integration of state-owned enterprises (SOEs) into a capitalist economic system is a delicate process. Policymakers should continue promoting market-oriented reforms within SOEs, encouraging competition, transparency, and efficiency. Privatization of certain sectors can also enhance their performance and contribute to overall economic growth.

The development of entrepreneurship and the private sector has been a key driver of China's economic success. Policymakers should foster a supportive ecosystem for entrepreneurs, such as providing access to capital, mentorship programs, and reducing bureaucratic red tape. Encouraging innovation and creativity will further strengthen the private sector's contribution to China's economy.

China's transition from a planned to a market economy has brought both challenges and opportunities. Policymakers should carefully navigate this transition, ensuring social stability, protecting vulnerable groups, and addressing environmental concerns. Emphasizing the rule of law, property rights, and strengthening institutions will be crucial in this process.

Innovation and technological advancements have propelled China's economic achievements. Policymakers and scholars must continue investing in research and development, fostering collaboration between academia, industry, and government. Encouraging a culture of innovation and protecting intellectual property rights will further enhance China's competitiveness on a global scale.

Globalization has significantly impacted China's economic experiment. Policymakers should continue embracing globalization while also safeguarding domestic industries and addressing income inequality. Strengthening international partnerships, promoting fair trade practices, and participating in global governance mechanisms will be essential for China's sustainable growth.

Income inequality and social disparities remain challenges in China's capitalist-communist hybrid system. Policymakers must implement measures to address these issues, such as redistributive policies, social safety nets, and promoting inclusive growth. Prioritizing education, healthcare, and social mobility can help reduce inequality and create a more equitable society.

The sustainability of China's economic model is a pressing concern. Policymakers and scholars should prioritize environmental sustainability, focusing on green technologies, renewable energy, and sustainable development practices. Balancing economic growth with environmental conservation will be crucial for China's long-term prosperity.

In conclusion, the lessons learned from China's economic experiment can provide valuable insights for economists, politicians, diplomats, and scholars. By considering the successes and challenges in areas such as market-oriented reforms, foreign investments, SEZs, SOEs, entrepreneurship, innovation, globalization, income inequality, and sustainability, policymakers can make informed decisions and recommendations for future development. The aim should be to create a balanced and inclusive economic model that drives growth while addressing social and environmental concerns.

Note: The formatting of sub-chapters may vary depending on the specific style guide or publishing requirements.

In this subchapter, we will explore the various aspects of the China Economic Experiment and how it has successfully utilized a capitalist economic system within a communist regime. This topic is of great interest to economists, politicians, diplomats, and scholars who are curious about the unique dynamics and achievements of China's economic model.

One of the key areas we will delve into is the successes of the China Economic Experiment. Despite the initial skepticism surrounding the compatibility of capitalism and communism, China has managed to achieve remarkable economic growth and development. We will highlight the specific factors that have contributed to this success and explore the lessons that can be learned from China's experience.

Market-oriented reforms have played a crucial role in China's economic growth. We will analyze the impact of these reforms, such as liberalizing trade, deregulating industries, and encouraging private entrepreneurship. These measures have helped China transition from a planned economy to a market economy, fostering innovation, competition, and efficiency.

Foreign investments have also been instrumental in China's economic transformation. We will examine how China strategically attracted and utilized foreign capital, technology, and expertise to drive its economic development. The role of Special Economic Zones (SEZs) will be explored in detail, as these designated areas played a pivotal role in attracting foreign investments and spurring economic growth.

The integration of state-owned enterprises (SOEs) into a capitalist economic system has been a complex process. We will analyze how China has managed to navigate this transition, balancing the need for efficiency and profitability while maintaining state control and social stability.

The development of entrepreneurship and the private sector has been a significant driver of China's economic success. We will highlight the policies and initiatives that have fostered the growth of this sector and examine the challenges and opportunities it presents.

China's transition from a planned to a market economy has not been without its challenges. We will explore the obstacles faced along the way, such as income inequality and social disparities. Furthermore, we will discuss the role of innovation and technological advancements in China's economic achievements and how globalization has influenced its economic experiment.

Finally, we will examine the sustainability of China's economic model and its implications for future development. As China's economic power continues to grow, understanding the long-term viability of its hybrid capitalist-communist system becomes increasingly important.

In conclusion, this subchapter will provide a comprehensive overview of the China Economic Experiment, showcasing its successes, challenges, and future prospects. It is an essential read for economists, politicians, diplomats, scholars, and anyone interested in understanding the unique dynamics of China's economic model.